INTHEFLOW

ENDORSEMENTS

Debbie Goodman-Bhyat has built the bridge between the hectic chaos of everyday business and the clarity and serenity that being present, and in the moment, brings. IntheFlow takes quite an ethereal concept and makes it practical for the businessperson to understand and, more importantly, to apply. The book is filled with wisdom and experience and will positively change the culture of businesses that apply its teachings to places of higher meaning and endow teams with more self-awareness and more empathy for fellow team members and clients alike.

Allon Raiz, CEO Raizcorp

There is no such thing as the absence of a corporate culture. In the absence of an intentional, deliberately cultivated culture, one develops only rarely what any leader would want. IntheFlow is a formula for creating not only a caring, gentle and thoughtful corporate culture, but a happier one. The best part is that it is a frank description of how Debbie made it work in her company – with remarkably little effort! This brief book will benefit any organisation's leader.

Ian Mann, MD, Gateways Business Consultants

This book is a downright provocative read that is honest, refreshing and energising, and speaks to the heart. This is a must-read for anyone and everyone who is seeking inner peace, joy, and genuine meaning and purpose in their personal and professional lives.

Professor Shirley Zinn, Group Head of Human Resources, Woolworths Holdings Ltd; and bestselling author of 'Swimming Upstream'

Work should be fun. Fulfilling at least beyond the achievements of the spreadsheet and endless pursuit of growth. Sooner or later even the hardest corporate animal will hit a wall. Debbie Goodman-Bhyat discovered 'mindfulness' under duress. Its principles didn't fall within the neat confines of what she regarded as her personal standards as a serial over-achiever. Great leaders, in my experience, never stop learning. They refuse to stagnate. By having the good sense to recognise that she was racing full-tilt at a concrete wall without a helmet, Debbie discovered the benefits of mindfulness. Her story could change yours. For the better.

Bruce Whitfield, Radio Host – 702

IntheFlow – Taking Mindfulness to Work by Debbie Goodman-Bhyat is both a personal and very practical book introducing readers to the technique of Mindfulnesses and its application in both personal and organisational life. Most notable is the author's journey in adopting and developing the practice despite her initial resistance and conceptual misgivings about the field. Having known Debbie for many years I can certainly vouch for this aspect of her story. The fact that she has managed to successfully follow this practice given her high-octane personality and commercial focus means that almost anyone (as she says) can do it. I was touched by the authenticity of the text. It is very readable. Highly recommended!

Marc Simon Kahn, Global Head of Human Resources and Organisation Development, Investec, and author of Coaching on the Axis.

Work is never just work. People have an interest in whether their workplace is healthy – in attitude, relationships and physically – and organisations have a matching interest in their people.

There are a LOT of self-help books out there for companies and individuals trying to improve. This one is a keeper. It's not too long, it's well written, including useful practical tools that are ambitious in their impact but not at all intimidating to get into. I suspect, like my other favourites *Allen Carr's Easy Way to Stop Smoking* and *The Tao of Coaching*, Debbie's short book will change behaviour more than most long ones.

Rob Dower, Chief Operating Officer and Director, Allan Gray Limited

First published in 2016

ISBN: 978-1-86922-632-9
ISBN: 978-1-86922-633-6 (ePDF)

Published by KR Publishing
P O Box 3954
Randburg
2125
Republic of South Africa

Tel: (011) 706-6009
Fax: (011) 706-1127
E-mail: orders@knowres.co.za
Website: www.kr.co.za

Printed and bound: HartWood Digital Printing, 243 Alexandra Avenue, Halfway House, Midrand
Typesetting, layout and design: Cia Joubert, cia@knowres.co.za
Cover design: Marlene de Villiers, marlene@knowres.co.za
Editing and proofreading: Valda Strauss, valda@global.co.za
Project management: Cia Joubert, cia@knowres.co.za

INTHEFLOW

Taking Mindfulness to Work

The power of noticing
the small stuff

by

Debbie Goodman-Bhyat

publishing

2016

DEDICATION

For Zaheer, Gianna and Malia.

I never knew my love for you could be this big.

ACKNOWLEDGEMENTS

I always love reading the acknowledgements page in books. It gives one real insight into all the work and effort, the support, collaboration, input and advice from those who help the author finally get their manuscript into print.

So, here goes ...

Writing *IntheFlow* has been a long journey for me. Frankly, if I hadn't been pressured into deadlines, I might still be editing and fixing. Because just when I think it's done, I re-read a bit, and discover that actually there's a slightly better way to phrase a paragraph, or explain a concept.

And as with all journeys, there are many people to acknowledge.

I'll start with my team at Jack Hammer, my adored 'work friends'. What a group of extraordinary people you are! Thank you to each one who has co-created *IntheFlow*, and enabled it to evolve into the wonderful, transformative ritual that it has become. Thank you for trusting me (even though you may have thought I was a little daft from time to time), and for being willing to share bits and pieces of your lives with me and with your colleagues.

Then, a big thank you to Shirley Zinn, author of *Swimming Upstream*, who generously introduced me to Wilhelm Crous of Knowledge Resources, publishers of *IntheFlow*. Shirley is known as an inspirational business leader, with accolades and achievements that will fill many pages. The accolades are all well-deserved. But what has touched me most is her unconditional kindness and open-heartedness. Tremendous!

Further acknowledgement to Margie Orford, prolific bestselling author, for some great advice along the way. My favourite Margie Orford comment is: 'Writing and editing never ends – you have embarked on an eternal journey of pain and self-doubt :)'. How true! Thank you for sharing your invaluable knowledge and experience.

And, Dr Simon Whitesman, Chairman of the Institute for Mindfulness South Africa. Simon has been my 'Mindfulness Coach' over the last few years, helping me to deepen my practice of Mindfulness. He also provided critical insights into my earlier versions of *IntheFlow*, which enabled me to sharpen my focus and make the necessary shifts with the book (although at the time, I was not particularly excited at the idea of another re-write!). Huge thanks to you, Simon, for your gentle guidance and support.

Now, for my mother. Who I know is so proud. And my dad who is no longer with us, but who I know would be equally proud. Thank you for your unconditional love, always. I love you.

And lastly, my 'four-family' (that's what my children call our 'unit'). My husband Zaheer and my daughters Gianna and Malia, who I treasure and adore beyond anything I could ever have imagined. I have written bits of this book on every family holiday we have taken for the last three years, and I can't wait to have a writing-free vacation. Thank you, my loves, for bringing meaning and purpose to my life, and for being my 'yesterday's best thing' every day. You are my everything.

TABLE OF CONTENTS

ABOUT THE AUTHOR

Debbie Goodman-Bhyat:

BA LLB; Entrepreneurial Growth Forum (London Business School)

CEO, Jack Hammer

Debbie is the founder and CEO of Jack Hammer, rated one of South Africa's top three executive search firms.

What drives her is an interest and investment in people and being able to identify greatness. Because great leaders grow great companies. Over 18 years she has done just that, building a team of impassioned people within Jack Hammer, and being instrumental in finding and securing key leaders at top companies and multinationals. Jack Hammer consults to some of the region's top blue-chip corporates, global multinationals and private enterprises, with a focus on senior management, executive and board-level appointments.

Her insights and stories have found their way into the media, where she appears regularly on television, radio and in print, and as a motivational speaker at conferences. She has published three leadership journals, with *IntheFlow – Taking Mindfulness to Work* being her first full non-fiction work.

Debbie's distinctive style and vision may come from her somewhat unconventional background. In her 'first' career, she was an award-winning contemporary dancer and choreographer ... while completing her law degree! Her great passion for kids (her own, as well as children in distress) and dance have an outlet in the Heart Projects she invests in through Jack Hammer.

Debbie is a founding member of the Cape Town chapter of EO, a global entrepreneurship organisation affiliated with YPO, and she is a trainer and facilitator for EO Global. She has recently been appointed to EO's MEPA Regional Council, as Forum Director.

She is married to Zaheer, a film producer, and they have two young daughters.

FOREWORD

IntheFlow – Taking Mindfulness to Work is an uplifting, eloquent and enlightening book that provokes us to discover the magic within ourselves so that we live more fulfilling lives.

It comes at a time of challenging economic dynamics, deep social and political challenges, fast-paced technological disruption and high demand on people and leaders to turn the treadmill up and move faster, with more balls in the air than ever. We have never-ending tick-boxes and to-do lists and we push ourselves hard to continue to deliver in a hugely stressful working environment. This is a dangerous cycle that deludes us into a belief that we are invincible and super out-performers in an ever-demanding world.

Like Debbie, I resonate with the paradox of feeling a sense of accomplishment knowing that I have concluded yet another piece of work on time and in budget, but a niggling feeling that this perfection and invincibility is not sustainable and does not lead to the deep personal fulfilment that is linked to a higher purpose and a life joyfully lived. Most of us do not smell the roses in the dizzying busy-ness to get things done, and pressure to make the bottom line, and we are missing out on the magic of life and what it truly has to offer us.

This book urges us to move to something new and improved that is exciting and deeply motivating – a path less taken. The thrust of the message is that small shifts can have a huge impact on our leadership style, on our team culture, on relationships, and on our productivity, performance and profitability. Yes, there is a bottom-line benefit to being more empathetic and trusting of people. Greater self-understanding and an awareness of our impact as leaders on others unlocks commitment, energy and effort.

This book is packed with enthusiasm about how we can change our lives for the better by providing us with tools, tips and practices that can impact our personal and professional lives. It offers anecdotes, principles, processes and philosophies that are accessible, simple and very powerful. It does so with wisdom, insight and humour that kept me riveted throughout the read.

Up till now, I have not used the word 'mindfulness'. But mindfulness is the essence of the book. I do believe that mindfulness is the biggest leadership challenge that we face given the Fourth Industrial Revolution of disruption and tectonic technological convergence that result in an 'always on' posture. How do we become more mindful in this frenetic world? How do we switch off the noise and the constant pinging, and listen to the finer notes? We have to learn to focus on what really matters and to know what depletes our energy. This book compels us to switch off the autopilot and to be truly present. It encourages us to notice our patterns and habits and to break the circuit and be present, to slow down enough so that we can speed up. It teaches us to value what really counts in life. It teaches about the effects of depletion of our energy and how to renew it.

Mindfulness is a way of life, not an event. Enjoy the read and the pearls of wisdom this book offers. I applaud the author for the leap of faith in writing this book and for sharing her unique insights that will enable us to live fulfilling and meaningful lives even in challenging times.

Professor Shirley Zinn, Group HR Director, Woolworths Holdings Limited

INTRODUCTION

Being an entrepreneur, CEO of a business and leader of teams, I spend most of my day at work – which has been my experimental 'lab' for assessing the benefits of IntheFlow. My dear colleagues and staff (otherwise known as my 'work friends') have been my 'lab rats', joining me in this daily ritual (our team has not missed a single day of practising IntheFlow in more than three years!).

Together, we have experienced a new kind of connectedness as a team, which has evolved over time into a truly special culture. We call it 'love and loyalty', and it encapsulates the trust, empathy, support and compassion that has developed amongst ourselves as a direct result of IntheFlow.

As you will discover as you read further, these great outcomes were actually quite unanticipated.

When I first designed IntheFlow, it was intended for my own personal use, as a way to help me become more 'present' on the journey of my life and to 'smell the roses' instead of constantly, relentlessly chasing towards goals, outcomes and end destinations.

I had begun to consider that instead of continuously, habitually pursuing the next big thing (because there's *always* another goal to aspire to), it might be quite wonderful to be able to pause for a few moments, and to take notice of things taking place right now, in the present.

It turns out that this is, actually, a pretty great way to live life. Which I discovered through practising IntheFlow – on my own initially.

So I shared it with my team. The transformation of our team culture – and our productivity – was incredible!

Now, I have a dream that one day we can all work in wonderful places, where we love to be, and where we can do our best work. The thing is – workspaces like these don't just 'happen'. They are co-created by people like you and me.

And if we (you and me) can all become a little more self-aware, a little less self-involved, a little more empathetic and a little more trusting, I believe that great work environments are within our reach.

It's not a 'magic bullet', but IntheFlow has the capacity to enhance the way we perceive – and experience – our lives, the way we work as teams, and as a result, our overall productivity and levels of performance.

How do I know? Well … let the story unfold.

PART 1

CULTIVATING SELF-AWARENESS

1 How did I get here?

It's a pretty sad story of all work and no play 'Makes Jack a Dull Boy' – or in my case, a dull girl.

My company (an executive search firm called Jack Hammer ... get it ... Jack?), my family (an amazing husband and two most magnificent and adorable daughters), my input into entrepreneurial and philanthropic initiatives, and more (I won't bore you at this early stage of the book with my list of commitments and responsibilities), require an intense focus to keep all these balls in the air.

And by the end of 2012, I was struggling.

I was working so hard at trying to ensure that the balls were all moving in perfect synchronisation that I was not only exhausted, but also quite miserable. And definitely not having any fun. At all.

Work was intense, I was grumpy and irritable at home, and I was pretty much dragging myself through each day with tremendous effort and strain. Complaining and moaning. The balls stayed in the air. But I was wiped out!

And then I went on holiday. Relief. Finally, a break.

Time to think, reflect and make some decisions. The first of which was that I was not going to have another year like this. Ever again.

There was a time, not so long ago, when work was fun, exhilarating, energising. There was a time when I did not feel like a dried-out washrag, when the hard work did not drain and sap my energy. So what happened between then and now?

And then the even bigger question – how on earth was I going to make a change? My family commitments were not going to reduce, my company and the work itself were not all of a sudden going to alter dramatically (sure, I could delegate a bit more, but the fundamentals would remain the same), and the demands of the other aspects of my life would also still be there.

I desperately wanted to experience the joy of work (and life) again!

Which led to the big realisation: The only thing that had any hope of significant change was ... ME! My outlook, my approach, my perspective, my experience of MY LIFE!

Aha – an epiphany! A pretty scary one because it meant that I needed to take the responsibility for making the change. Anything external would merely be 'tweaks' and would ultimately never be sustainable or have lasting impact.

As my mother would say ... 'Oy Vey!'

So my search began. The hardest part of which was that I was not entirely sure what I was looking for.

But I had a lot of questions. Mostly around: 'How come, in spite of all the good things happening in my life, I'm focusing on the stuff that's mostly not great (in other words, I'm seeing the murky mud instead of the joy and light)?' As well as: 'I seem to be chasing goals and achievements all the time – how can I pause long enough to enjoy the journey?' And: 'What do I need to do to change my perceptions and experience of my life?'

Apparently, asking the right questions is the first step to finding solutions. There is a famous quote by Rilke: 'Be patient toward all that is unsolved in your heart and try to love the questions themselves.'[1] Which sounds like a great state of being to aspire to – but for me, extremely challenging to accept. I really like solutions. Preferably quick ones.

It turns out that the questions I had started to ask had no quick fixes – but at least they lead me to my first important discovery.

Which was a book that had been sitting on my shelf for a while. Ignored, unread, gathering a bit of dust as benched books tend to do, regardless of how good the housekeeping. It had been gifted to me by my husband who, several months prior to my miraculous 'discovery', had noted my accumulating stress, overwhelming fatigue and general malaise, and had sourced the book on my behalf.

With the auspicious title, *Mindfulness – A Practical Guide to Finding Peace in a Frantic World*, by Mark Williams and Danny Penman,[2] I had shelved it due to my self-proclaimed insistence that I was 'handling things just fine', and attributing my stress to the millions of balls in the air that I was juggling – to my mind, with great finesse, actually!

The initial book toss was also due to a quick perusal (I at least had to do that considering the 'gifted' nature of the item) where the words 'meditation' and 'breathing' jumped out at me, causing instinctive rejection. Firstly, I knew how to breathe. Secondly, I had neither the time nor the inclination to take on even one more thing in my day, especially something like 'meditation', which seemingly offered absolutely no productive output whatsoever.

In fact, I had tried meditation a couple of times previously in yoga classes, and had found it terribly boring and frustrating. I wanted to do it 'right', but the yoga teacher gave only the most basic of directions, and I had no idea if I was doing the meditation successfully. Which at the time was very important to me.

So, with all of these preconceived ideas and notions, I had accepted the gift graciously (I hope), which was clearly offered with love and the best intentions, and then put it aside ... for rediscovery at a more appropriate time. (You know the saying: "When the student is ready, the teacher will appear"?)

Turns out, the appropriate time was early in 2013.

I was on a red-eye flight to Johannesburg, and as I was walking out the door, I hastily grabbed a book to read on board and shoved it in my bag. It was only when I pulled it out as we became airborne that I realised I had brought 'the book'. I rolled my eyes to myself, looked desperately for some other reading material, and with my choices being the in-flight mag and *Mindfulness* ..., I surrendered to the latter.

In hindsight, I must also thank the airline for an extremely dreary airline mag. Who knows where my destiny would have lead should the magazine have offered sufficiently engaging reading. Needless to say, my fate unfolded before me as I turned the pages of what was soon to become my tome of wisdom.

By the time the flight landed, I had completed the introductory chapters and my first Mindfulness meditation. I was hooked, and taking on the very accessible eight-week Mindfulness programme was an inevitability – the only requirement being the commitment to daily practice.

Which, let me be frank, was not entirely without its challenges. Finding time was never going to be possible. So **making** time for the daily meditations became a critical priority.

I guess I kept it up because I could feel the benefits almost instantly (yes, I enjoy experiencing a fast – preferably immediate, if I'm to be totally honest – connection between endeavour and reward), and because the ideas and principles of Mindfulness really resonated with me and offered some insights to the 'life questions' I had begun to ask.

2 Mindfulness – it's everywhere!

As my exploration with Mindfulness began to unfold, I became more and more aware of how Mindfulness literature seemed to be popping up all over the show (or perhaps it's like when you buy – or aspire to buy – a certain type of car, and all of a sudden you see hundreds of exactly the same car all over the roads).

Needless to say, Mindfulness is nowadays part of common discourse and lexicon – books and journals abound on the topic itself in its 'purist' form (Jon Kabat-Zinn, Mark Williams, Matthieu Ricard, Thich Nhat Hanh ... the list is long and inspiring), as well as in derivative literature and magazine articles ('Thrive' by Ariana Huffington, *Newsweek*, *The Times*, *Huffington Post*, et al).

And even if you've not encountered any of this literary material, Mindfulness terminology will almost certainly have permeated your consciousness (or subconscious) in one way or another. A short perusal of most Facebook feeds reveals quotes and 'daily inspirations' connected to Mindfulness; and instantly downloadable, free Mindfulness apps[1] are available at the click of a button.

---

1 Some good Mindfulness apps include: 'Headspace'; 'The Mindfulness App'; 'Stop, Breathe & Think'.

So the material is out there in abundance. But gaining a handle on what Mindfulness 'is', is not an easy quest. Even trying to find a definition of Mindfulness is tough, so here's the most succinct, 'in-a-nutshell' description available, from the most credible source, the pioneer himself, Jon Kabat-Zinn:

'The awareness which arises when we pay attention, on purpose, without judgement, to the experience of the present moment, in the service of insight, wisdom and compassion.'

It's a beautiful, simple sentence. And when I read it for the first time, I did not understand its meaning at all! I mean, I understood the words, but missed the essence completely, and it's taken a long time to gain enough insight (and courage) to offer further explanation and expansion on this iteration.

And it has taken nerves of steel to write a book about a Mindfulness-based programme which I developed, as a relative beginner in the practice and then introduced into my company – as an experiment.

A good one, it turns out!

Nonetheless, as I offer my personal thoughts on the topic of Mindfulness, my caveat is that I do not consider myself an 'expert'. I am not a teacher of eight-week Mindfulness programmes, I am not an academic, a scientist or a clinician, and I certainly have not reached any lofty heights of wisdom or enlightenment.

I am, however, a practitioner. With the emphasis on 'practice' and 'practical'. I practice Mindfulness meditation daily. And 'IntheFlow', the programme I developed for my company, is a simple and practical way of practising principles of Mindfulness during one's day, when one is 'off the cushion'.

3 Mindfulness 101

Before we move on further – the basics about Mindfulness: Jon Kabat-Zinn (PhD, Professor of Medicine Emeritus) is widely regarded as the pioneer of the Mindfulness 'movement' and the founder of MBSR (Mindfulness-based stress reduction), establishing the Centre of Mindfulness at the University of Massachusetts Medical School, and author of some great books on the topic. My top picks are *Full Catastrophe Living*,[3] *Mindfulness for Beginners*,[4] and *Wherever You Go, There You Are.*[5]

Mindfulness-based practices and techniques are nowadays widely used in a range of environments. They are recognised tools in the treatment of depression and mental illness as well as other pathology. They have been successfully used in prisons, schools and in private- and public-sector organisations all over the world.

Because, according to the studies that have taken place over the last decade or so, practising Mindfulness can help improve one's resilience[6] and response to stress;[7] as well as significantly increase the base level of one's happiness.[8]

Whilst not always overtly stated in the secular material on the topic, there are connections between Buddhist principles and Mindfulness, with both exploring qualities of the mind and heart as a key foundation. Mindfulness can nevertheless be practised in an entirely faith-agnostic manner – and in fact, this is one of the key attractions for me.

Most likely, because of the flexibility of the practice to take on a tone that is more or less spiritual or secular, depending on the teacher and the students, Mindfulness has wide appeal and accessibility.

Mindfulness programmes and practices have been incorporated in some form or another (either full eight-week programmes, or meditation sessions, typically) into some high-profile organisations, including Google, Intel, Aetna, Keurig Green Mountain, Target and more.

The objectives being to enable employees to deal with stress and anxiety better, to improve their sense of wellness, EQ and compassion, to be more focused – and thereby increase productivity and performance.

Frankly, IntheFlow – the programme I introduced to Jack Hammer and the key subject matter of this book – was initially intended to do the same. Enhance productivity. My own and my team's.

What I discovered over time was that this was merely the tip of the iceberg.

And I can't wait to tell you about the rest of the iceberg. But first, some key principles of Mindfulness.

Don't just scan this next chapter. It's important, and I will attempt to be brief.

4 The key principles of Mindfulness

'The awareness which arises when we pay attention, on purpose, without judgement, to the experience of the present moment, in the service of insight, wisdom and compassion.'

Despite my best attempts, I can't come up with anything more articulate than this one-liner to define Mindfulness.

But just because it's a great sentence, doesn't mean that it's easy to understand, so I'm going to offer some interpretation regarding the key principles, which (in no specific order), include the following:

- focus and attention to the present ('being')
- awareness of sensation, emotion and thought
- acceptance (which is NOT the same as 'giving up')
- appreciation
- loving kindness and compassion
- non-judgement
- non-striving

The list is probably longer, but I'll cap it here – with some commentary.

Firstly, on 'being' – a concept that almost caused several temper tantrums (mine) due to my absolute lack of understanding of what on earth 'being' meant. How do you 'do' it? Aren't we in any case 'being' by just living?

Apparently not.

As evidenced by the fact that I had been 'living' for sure, but racing from one deadline to the next, trying to fit in as much as possible into the day, focusing on getting to the end of projects, achieving targets and ticking boxes on my to-do list. My focus was on the destination, with very limited attention to the journey, and even less consciousness or awareness of the small, not-particularly-special, but nevertheless wonderful, moments along the way.

I'd been doing the 'living', but not much of the 'being' – which can be described as 'experiencing, sensing, noticing and appreciating the present'. And which is possible only if one's mind can focus on the present and bring attention and awareness to 'now'.

'Being' may sound quite simple ... but for me, it was NOT simple at all. I typically have a racing mind which, left alone for more than a second, will be off on its own tangent, thinking a million thoughts about work, kids, husband, budgets, my team, my clients, the broken curtain in my daughter's room ...

Now this is apparently completely normal and natural activity for minds. But doesn't help if one is trying to 'be'. Aagghh!

So the big deal about Mindfulness practice is that the 'training' offers the opportunity to learn how to focus the mind on the present, to become aware of the times when the mind has gone off on its own meander, and to (gently and compassionately) shift the mind back to the present to enable one to 'BE'.

And yes, this is 'training' – just like toning muscles, Mindfulness practice provides training for the mind to keep coming back from its random wandering to the present.

Note also my parentheses-enclosed phrase: 'Gently and compassionately'. This describes the qualitative aspect of Mindfulness practice which – in becoming aware that your mind has wandered off – encourages you to simply usher your awareness back to the present, without self-judgement or recrimination. No lambasting around being right or wrong (oh boy, another tough one for me!); instead, just letting the thoughts be, with a feeling tone of loving kindness and compassion for oneself.

All of which were qualities and emotions that I was particularly unskilled at tapping into in the early days, and frankly still struggle with from time to time. I wanted every meditation to be awesome, I wanted to experience a sense of achievement, of doing things right, of progressing in my practice – be it a sense of peacefulness or calm, or just the ability to focus on my breathing without distraction for the count of 10.

And when these outcomes were not fulfilled, or my mind kept wandering, or I was unable to settle into any kind of breathing rhythm ... well, I would berate myself, or criticise myself in some way or another.

Completely opposite to the ideas of compassion and non-judgement.

And which thankfully, over time, I have found so much easier. My mind still does its dance whenever it feels like it, but I get a lot less irritated and annoyed with it. In fact, these days I'm (mostly) quite gentle with my mind – and myself.

Another (and last for now) of the key principles that I'd like to mention – because it bothered me for the longest time – is the idea of 'non-striving' (which is inter-related with paying attention to the present, or 'being').

This really confused me. As an avid goal-setter and goal-achiever, I just couldn't get my head around this! Non-striving just seemed so apathetic (and pathetic, in my view), because almost everything I have accomplished has been due to deciding what I want, why I want it and then making plans and strategies to achieve this.

Over the years, I have been an unashamed fan of motivational 'gurus'. My 'hall of fame' includes Anthony Robbins (a particular favourite of mine is his RPM Programme,[9] an incredibly well-structured programme targeted towards achieving goals through great planning), Brian Tracy's (*Goals!*),[10] and Jack Canfield (of *Chicken Soup for the Soul* fame),[11] a guru on success strategies who could motivate even the laziest sod on earth.

So imagine my frustration and perplexity with a concept like 'non-striving'!

What took me some time to 'get', was that the concept of non-striving did not preclude, negate or diminish any endeavour towards achievement, goals or success.

Instead, this principle offers the opportunity to 'be'. To be present. To be 'now'. To be here. To give our full attention, perhaps only for a few moments, to where we actually are.

Which is what I wanted, and needed, in order to make the changes I was looking for in the first place (remember the washed-out rag woman I described in the first chapter?).

What I began to realise is that we miss the present – the journey – when we are in 'striving' mode and focused primarily on outcomes. And so I befriended the concept of 'non-striving', whilst simultaneously continuing to drive towards my goals. The two are not mutually exclusive – but the latter, without the former, leaves me feeling empty.

I choose, therefore, to be as achievement oriented as I like, but to remind myself daily through the principle of non-striving to 'smell the roses'.

5 Taking Mindfulness to work

Having experienced the benefits of Mindfulness meditations personally, I wanted to share Mindfulness with everyone! In particular, the people I spend most of my time with – my team at work.

And so I started wondering whether I, too (like the Googles of the world), could introduce this into my business.

Like the large multinationals who have introduced Mindfulness practice into their organisations in order to help employees reduce stress and anxiety, increase focus and attention, and ultimately enhance productivity, surely my team at Jack Hammer could benefit too?

And further, how about cultivating my levels of compassion and empathy as a leader, to enhance relationships with my employees and develop a culture of acceptance, tolerance, trust and connectedness?

I started researching the benefits of meditation and was blown away by the plethora of material showing the extraordinary effects of regular meditation on everything from reduced stress levels, to improved concentration and resilience, and increased levels of emotional intelligence and overall mental health.

Meditation has also been proven to increase feelings of happiness[12] – and the correlation between happiness and work productivity is irrefutable. Reduced absenteeism, increased output, creativity and innovation are all documented as outcomes that result from a sense of well-being and happiness.

I attended a seminar a few years ago in Nepal, and had the privilege of meeting Matthieu Ricard, Buddhist monk, author and photographer, who is reportedly the 'happiest man on earth'.[13]

His presentation at the conference impacted me profoundly, with one of the big 'aha's' being his explanation around the shifts in brain physiology after just a few weeks of meditating for ten minutes per day.

To my right is Matthieu Ricard, who joined my husband and me in a helicopter trip to view the peak of Everest, in March 2013. It was the first time I'd ever met a Tibetan monk (well, actually any monk), and I was awed at how down-to-earth and 'accessible' he was.

Suffice to say, the effects and beneficial outcomes of meditation (whether using Mindfulness-based meditation techniques or any other) are unquestionable. The research proves it. Anecdotally, I can personally vouch for it.

So the logical next step would have been to incorporate it into my organisation, to figure out when, where and how I could include daily meditation as part of our work day in order to cultivate an environment with happy, optimally productive people.

Brilliant idea (albeit not entirely original).

In theory.

Because as I started to unpack this in my head, bit by bit, I realised that there were a couple of challenges I would need to address.

6 The road blocks to the plan

Some of these issues were logistical, practical ones. Like: What time of day would meditation sessions take place? Who would lead them? Many of my team members work remotely, and even the ones who are in the office seldom keep to regular schedules. We work in a very flexible manner, with people in and out the office depending on meetings, travel schedules or home and domestic commitments.

So a daily, group meditation session would be pretty tough to arrange and then stick to with our respective erratic schedules.

And one thing I know about introducing a new practice, exercise or plan to a team – it needs to be scheduled, regular, and then upheld if it is to have any hope of gaining traction, sustaining and then having the impact for which it was introduced in the first place.

Having designed hundreds of incentive schemes and reward offers for my business development teams, with varying degrees of success (and some outright failures), I can say with certainty that very regular (preferably daily) reminders and prompts are integral to sustaining a new practice of any sort in an organisation.

Even the greatest ideas and sky-high motivation levels are doomed to plummet if there isn't a system of periodic, deliberate, planned reinforcement of some sort.

Certainly, with something like meditation, its impact is only felt when it is practised for a certain amount of time, regularly every day, for an extended period.

So the practicalities of daily meditation sessions for my team – though not insurmountable – were a key consideration. The more important issues for me, however, were some ideological, philosophical ones.

The first of which was a concern about 'imposing' meditation practice onto a group of people who might be quite resistant to the idea. I was aware of how 'esoteric' or foreign the concept and practice of meditation is to many people. I had seen how long I had taken to come around to the idea, and how vehemently (and instinctively) I had rejected meditation. I was also cognisant that for people who observe a religious faith, the spiritual aspects of meditation might conflict in some way with their religious practice.

I tried out a basic breathing exercise with my team one day and saw one of my more religious colleagues become extremely uncomfortable. Afterwards she explained that it just felt 'wrong' to her, as this type of contemplative quiet was 'reserved for prayer with God'.

The second of these – and probably the most important of all – was around my own challenges of applying the key principles of Mindfulness beyond my meditation sessions.

Although 'hooked' almost instantly from my first Mindfulness programme, I seemed unable to transition my developing sense of awareness of my thoughts, feelings and sensations from my meditation practice to the rest of my day. I was slowly cultivating the ability to bring my attention to my breath and my body, and to feel present instead of distracted – but the moment I was 'off the cushion', it was back to the old patterns.

I was either not trying hard enough … or perhaps I needed something else.

7 How do you change the hard-wiring?

Let's take a quick side-step, to explain a bit more about Mindfulness and meditation. Firstly, there are many different types and styles of meditation, and Mindfulness meditation is but one – with its own unique style, pace, rituals, tone and content.

Mindfulness as an over-arching practice **includes** meditation, which is the 'formal' part of Mindfulness. Beyond the meditation bit, every other waking moment can be experienced mindfully – or, in other words, Mindfulness (present moment awareness) is available on or off the cushion, during, before and after meditation.

Now, while I was making progress during my formal meditation practice, I was still struggling to pay attention and bring awareness to the 'here and now' of my day. I was trying to cultivate the ability to 'be present' and notice elements of my day that would usually be ignored because they were neither particularly spectacular nor terribly awful, but I was still defaulting to my well-rehearsed pattern of churning through my day on autopilot.

This meeting, next meeting, take a call, deal with emails, schedule, arrange, plan, sort ... all on overdrive in order to squeeze everything in and get ... exactly where? To the end of the day?

I was STILL motoring through my day, rushing madly from one thing to the next, slashing my list of 'to-do-today' items, but not really taking the time to notice anything at all. STILL way too focused on the destination, and having a hard time being present during the journey of the day.

So the big question now was how to change the hard-wiring and shift the Mindfulness principles from a relatively 'structured' meditation session to the fluidity (veering on chaos) of the work day.

I use the word 'structured' because a Mindfulness meditation session is typically organised as follows: decide to meditate, move into meditation position (sitting on a chair or cushion, lying down for a body-scan-style meditation, or the start position for a movement meditation), commence the meditation, complete the meditation.

That's not to say that this is the only way – certainly, one could meditate on a train, bus or aeroplane (I have), standing waiting in a queue (I have found this to be good use of time) and other similar non-conventional situations.

But for the most part, meditation typically happens in a 'structured-ish' way.

Which is not how most days work – even if one leads a very routine-like existence. Most days consist of a bunch of unknown, unplanned and unanticipated variables and moving parts that take us away from 'being' and automatically shove us into acting and reacting on pure autopilot.

In addition, during meditation, it's just oneself and one's own mind and body to deal with. The rest of the day it's not like that at all! Most of us are communicating and interacting with others all day long, in some form or another (via email, phone, face-to-face meetings, social media) – and it's often here that we encounter our challenges.

Irritation, annoyance, frustration, judgement, blame, anger, embarrassment – for me, these typically arise in my interactions and engagements with others. And not that I'm a generally irritable person (well, I don't think I am, although you might need to speak to my nearest and dearest about that), but this range of emotion seldom happens in a vacuum.

And it's these types of feelings that are the ones that distract our minds and challenge our ability to be present. To pay attention to the small, special moments that may simultaneously be occurring, but which we fail to notice because our minds are elsewhere ... preoccupied, absorbed, far away.

If most of our working days are like this, then the hard-wiring will likely be ingrained (as was mine), and any good intentions to try to be more present and aware of the positive (or negative), good (or bad) special moments are likely to fly out the window as soon as one gets embroiled in the events of the day.

I realised that in order to shift the default patterns and actually apply Mindfulness principles to the regular course of my day – being present, paying focused attention to the 'now', nurturing an awareness of the special moments happening in my life and cultivating greater compassion for myself and others – I needed to develop some kind of daily ritual which would hopefully become a 'habit', and which would enable the transition I was trying to make.

And this 'ritual' would need to be something other than formal meditation practice – (which I continue to do each day and highly recommend to every human being as an essential life tool).

And thus: IntheFlow

8 IntheFlow – a way to practise Mindfulness

Let me start this chapter by reiterating that IntheFlow is NOT a 'pure' Mindfulness programme. In fact, it differs substantially from most Mindfulness programmes that have been incorporated into work environments in that it does not include formal meditation practice.

After reading *Work* by Thich Nhat Hanh,[14] Zen master, global spiritual leader, peace activist and bestselling author on Mindfulness, I must admit to feeling very conflicted about not incorporating meditation or breathing exercises as fundamental and integral elements of IntheFlow.

Work presents some wonderful, practical ideas for incorporating Mindfulness-based exercises, including the recitation of *gathas*, breathing and other meditations throughout the day.

I particularly love this morning *gatha*:

Waking up this morning, I smile. Twenty-four brand-new hours are before me. I vow to live fully each moment and to look at all beings with eyes of compassion.

And then, another good read, *Search Inside Yourself*, by Chade Meng Tan,[15] describes the MBSR programme and Search Inside Yourself curriculum, which has been established at Google headquarters (with the objective of developing the EQ of Google employees at work and at home).

The curriculum was developed in collaboration with Jon Kabat-Zinn and is highly acclaimed by teachers in the 'industry' as well as participants. Apparently, there are long waiting lists to join the programme.

Yet, despite these great examples, which led to lots of second-guessing myself about not including meditation as part of IntheFlow, I am clear about this decision. IntheFlow is a modified, adapted Mindfulness-based programme. It is not purist and it also includes elements that are not Mindfulness-based at all.

Further, IntheFlow is not a substitute for meditation. In an ideal world, those who practise IntheFlow will also meditate daily. But my view is that they should come to the decision to meditate on their own.

In fact, several of my employees have done so. Having been exposed to the Mindfulness principles through IntheFlow, they have independently decided to follow their own eight-week Mindfulness programmes and have commenced regular meditation practice.

Of their own accord.

9 So ... does it work?

It's a valid question. And a good one to ask at this stage as there's still a fair portion of this book to complete, and why bother if the intended outcomes don't materialise as promised?

Specifically, the questions might be: Has IntheFlow had a positive impact on me personally? Have I managed to cultivate an awareness of the present moment, enabling an appreciation of my 'journey' and enhanced self-awareness? Has it shifted my leadership style? Have my staff experienced change in their personal lives, or in their work productivity? Has our company culture gone through a transformation? And has IntheFlow influenced the organisation's bottom line?

The answer, specifically, and in a nutshell, is YES (or else this would be a much shorter book).

Out of the nutshell, the answer is more complex and much less succinct:

Looking back after the first year of introducing IntheFlow to my business, I can say without any hesitation that it was one of the best years of my life, both personally and professionally.

Personally, I achieved some goals and aspirations I had never imagined were possible and, more importantly (because achieving goals has never been a shortcoming), I found myself experiencing the process and steps towards the goals with a real sense of joy and fulfilment.

What had previously eluded me – the ability to enjoy and appreciate the journey as opposed to just the outcome – now became possible, with ease. Washed-out rag woman (me, a year earlier) became a distant memory.

And in cultivating my personal awareness of the present, I started to become more self-aware. Which, of course, impacted every area of my life – but most notably at work.

In my professional domain, I truly stepped into my role as a leader, making some significant changes, particularly in the quality of my engagement with my staff.

This was a turning point for me. I found myself shifting into a zone of compassionate leadership, which ultimately paved the way for the cultivation of a company culture of 'love and loyalty'.

But a 'company culture' is completely dependent on the people in the company and how they are experiencing their lives at work (and at home). No matter how much pivoting I did as a leader, the only way to impact culture was for everyone in the organisation to be part of co-creating it.

Which they did. IntheFlow was – and is – integral to our magnificent culture of generosity, empathy, trust and support. It enables the teams to connect in a new way, to share more openly and authentically, and to see one another with the perspective of compassion and understanding.

And just in case you think I'm avoiding the question about 'the bottom line', here's the answer to that: during the first year of practising IntheFlow, we experienced more than 20% growth in revenue.

So, to repeat, YES, IntheFlow most definitely works!

But, has there been no stress at all, has it all been smooth-sailing, have I not been a horrible boss on occasion, have I had zero staff turnover and perfect performance from everyone consistently?

Are you kidding? Of course I've been anxious, and angry, and irritable, and dismissive, and completely lacking in empathy from time to time. My employees have had their ups and downs too, and we've had people come and go who did not crack the high standards or fit in with the culture.

We've all had days when it's been so chaotic and crazy that stopping for even a few minutes to practise IntheFlow seemed impossible. And there have been months when we've missed our targets, or were unable to achieve sky-rocketing productivity.

Because that is the reality of life! And from time to time, things go horribly wrong, and each one of us can have a lousy day.

The joy of IntheFlow is that we get to notice, appreciate and be present to what's happening – even if it's just for a few moments – every day (including the not-so-great ones).

Now, the direct causal link between IntheFlow and revenue growth is impossible to prove – but the research has already been done elsewhere, and the data shows unequivocally that people who feel respected and trusted in their work environments are happier, less anxious and perform at their best. Overlay this with the cultivation of personal self-awareness and empathy for ones colleagues, and you have substantially increased productivity and high-quality delivery.

So, despite the lack of scientific data proving that IntheFlow has had anything at all to do with all the pretty fantastic things that started to happen for me , my staff and our company, I can offer this as some 'food for thought':

The 'stuff' I was doing pre- and post-IntheFlow has not changed much. My life is as busy and has as many (if not more) variables to consider and manage. I still have many, many balls in the air.

But – and this is a BIG BUT – I have had a remarkably different perception, experience and appreciation of my life before and after commencing IntheFlow.

As have my staff and those outside of Jack Hammer (entrepreneurs, corporate employees and other groups) who have been introduced to IntheFlow and have tried it out.

And we can't all be wrong!

10 The graveyard of great ideas

The thing is, anything new that one tries to introduce into one's life – a diet, an exercise programme, drinking more water, taking vitamins and supplements, date night with your spouse ... you know, all the periodic 'resolutions' we try to follow – typically start out with some enthusiasm, and then die a slow (or fast) death.

I call it 'the graveyard of great ideas'.

Because too few of the positive new habits we want to cultivate to improve our lives, or to support a healthier way of being, gain much traction or stick around for the long term.

How come?

Because change of any sort is hard, regardless of how great the benefits. And without a very practical, easy-to-follow, well-supported programme, it's really challenging to stick with something new, so that it has enough time to become a ritual, and then eventually a habit.

Having read hundreds of books and attended many talks and presentations by some of the most outstanding speakers on topics related to 'change' – life, love, career, leadership, friends, money … the list is endless – I can say with some authority that the notion of change itself, shifting towards something 'new and improved' is inspiring, intoxicating at times, and certainly highly motivational.

In other words, I get really excited by new ideas, and want to try them out. Immediately.

And they seem so feasible. 'Ten easy steps to X'. 'The 5 plan approach to Y'. 'The 25 principles to Z'.

Even when not presented quite so glibly (no disrespect to the motivational gurus, some of whose material I enjoy and admire), new ideas are typically introduced with the assumption that they will be easy to implement.

But they're not! You leave the conference with the manual, and with great intentions to study it again when you have some time, but that never happens, right? Even if – like me – you take copious notes with a list of action items to follow up after the presentation or seminar or workshop, the likelihood of this actually happening is not particularly high.

It could just be me … but I doubt so.

And so ultimately, all the energy and excitement expended over a new idea, something that could significantly (or even just minimally) enhance one's life, dwindles into nothingness.

It was with this awareness that I designed IntheFlow, knowing that the chances of it actually gaining traction in my business (or anyone else's) and making the impact for which it was intended (or any positive impact at all, even unintended benefits would be great) was actually quite low.

Unless it was really simple to understand, truly easy – and enjoyable – to execute and very well-supported with prompts and reminders.

Which it is.

Really.

And I can say this with absolute conviction because at the time of writing, my company has been following IntheFlow for more than three years. Every single work day.

Which is approximately 756 days. And counting.

And whether you're on your own or part of a group, no ritual can be sustained for that long unless it has these fundamental characteristics:

- it's simple to understand (complexity is a killer)
- it's easy to follow (no special tools or technology required, and it doesn't take much time)
- it adds value (regardless of the ease or simplicity, if there are insufficient gains, no way will it have longevity)

IntheFlow is all of the above.

And the point of this book is to offer you a step-by-step guide to the 'how', so that once you've read the last page, you'll immediately be able to start practising it.

Because what a pity if you take the time to read this whole thing, get excited by the ideas, and then ... nothing?

The graveyard?

Not on my watch!

11 IntheFlow – the cost benefit ratio

I've mentioned it already, but it's worth repeating:

One of the greatest things about IntheFlow, is that it is really, really, really, really easy to include into your day.

Now, I've been told that I have a tendency towards hyperbole.

But I'm really not exaggerating.

Really.

In fact, of all the million and one things I squish into my twenty-four hours, it is the simplest and quickest – but with the greatest impact, considering the time it takes.

So if you're the analytical type, the cost to benefit ratio is impressive!

Which, as I write, I realise comes across as a bit of a schmoozy, salesy statement.

After all, when was the last time you learned something new, that had the potential for profound influence on your life, and did not involve pain, deprivation or significant discomfort?

Never, right? Unless it was a scam, or some kind of quick-fix nonsense with no substance or sustainability.

I have heard the saying 'no gain without pain' my whole life, and I'm part of a generation that still believes in the value and benefit of hard work and sacrifice in order to derive pleasure. So, I don't blame you if you're feeling somewhat sceptical about anything that promises great benefits with ease and simplicity.

So I'd like to repeat the 'simple and easy' bit, but with a caveat:

Firstly, IntheFlow is very simple to understand. In fact, some feedback from a webinar I conducted a while back noted that the delegates felt IntheFlow was too 'simplistic'. (They had clearly been expecting something more complex with a lot more obfuscating jargon, or some challenging infographics, perhaps.)

Secondly, IntheFlow is very easy to implement. There are no 'tech' tools beyond email, and no training is required beyond the initial explanation of the system. Which you will find in this book.

Thirdly, IntheFlow involves no pain or discomfort. It will not take up loads of time (a few minutes of your day, max), or cost more money, or be overly demanding of you in any way.

But (here's the caveat) it does require discipline. To do it every day. Or at least every work day.

If you can manage just that – regularity – then the benefits of IntheFlow will materialise. Quickly.

And that's not a sales schpiel.

12 What you pay attention to really matters

Within a few weeks of commencing my daily IntheFlow ritual, I was feeling lighter, brighter and ... happier. Much less frazzled and stressed out, and much more able to cope with the inevitable curve-balls of the day.

Client issues, staff hassles, family dramas ... they were all still there, but in a short space of time, I found myself handling it all with much greater ease. Because I now had a counter-balance with IntheFlow which helped me to start paying attention to moments in my day that had previously received little or no attention.

These 'moments' were neither particularly dramatic, nor overly exciting. In fact, for the most part, they were just kind of ordinary. Hence the prior inattention. But now, with the prompts from IntheFlow that guided me to apply focus and awareness to aspects of my life that would not usually have found a spotlight at all, my perspectives about my day started to shift and change.

Because what you pay attention to really matters.

It affects your mood and your state of being, and defines your reality.

It affects your approach and response to the events and people around you.

Which in turn impacts the outcomes of every single interaction.

And by cultivating the ability to pay attention and bring awareness to moments other than those that typically fight for and demand our attention (the fear or novelty-based ones), IntheFlow can significantly impact one's perceptions, one's emotions and one's experiences.

But don't just take my word for it.

Here are a few comments from the team at Jack Hammer:

> "With IntheFlow, I am aware of my day, appreciating and creating a positive flow of energy into my daily life." (Senior executive search consultant)

> "This exercise has made me more aware of how fortunate I am, despite the bumps in the road, and spurred me to influence those in my life to see the positive aspects of any situation. My perception of life has become much lighter, and more conscious." (Principal researcher)

> "It puts you in a better, happy 'zone', and gives you that feeling of being 'in the flow'. It's amazing in its simplicity, and only takes a minute or two, first thing in the morning." (Executive consultant)

What started happening with my team when they first started practising IntheFlow, is that they all of a sudden had a daily prompt to start paying attention to parts of their day that they had previously not given a moment's notice.

Their lives and their days did not go through some kind of miraculous transition – just their awareness did.

Such a small shift – a change of awareness – was (and is) able to make such a great impact.

Which is why what you pay attention to really matters. In fact, paying attention AT ALL really matters.

Here is a quotation by famous Scottish psychiatrist, R.D. Laing:

> 'The range of what we think and do is limited by what we fail to notice. And because we fail to notice that we fail to notice, there is little we can do to change; until we notice how failing to notice shapes our thoughts and deeds.'[16]

And on that quite philosophical note, I'll bring this chapter to a close.

13 Here it is – IntheFlow!

So, here we are, after much preamble (yes, I've managed to get you all the way to chapter 13), and finally I'm going to share IntheFlow with you.

IntheFlow consists of six 'prompts' that awaken us to the ordinary – yet special – moments of our lives, by paying attention, on purpose, to these moments.

The six prompts are:

1. Yesterday's Best Thing

2. Grateful For

3. Looking Forward To

4. Conscious Kindness

5. Compliment Sincerely

6. Greet Warmly

These prompts enable the development our awareness of small, ordinary moments that are taking place in our lives, every day.

The small stuff. And the big stuff. But mostly the small stuff.

In *Full Catastrophe Living*, Jon Kabat-Zinn has this to say about 'the small stuff':

> 'Not only does the small stuff matter. The small stuff isn't so small. It turns out to be huge. Tiny shifts in viewpoint, in attitude, and in your efforts to be present can have enormous effects on your body, on your mind and in the world'.[17]

I've experienced this first hand.

By becoming aware of the small stuff happening in my day, through the prompts that help me shift out of 'autopilot', I have developed greater awareness of the present, as well as enhanced self-awareness.

This in turn has resulted in a consciousness of well-being and a sense of vitality. (Which I guess is what happens when you stop to smell the roses.)

And, when IntheFlow is practised with a team in the work environment, it enables each individual to develop this awareness too.

The impact of IntheFlow is further enhanced through a simple communication tool which connects teams at work, cultivating compassion and empathy, relationships of trust and support, and (if you're really lucky) a culture of love and loyalty.

And we all know that when people are working in great work environments, they perform optimally.

Now, I get that this may all sound a little too good to be true. And I agree – if I was working in an average-to-awful team environment, I might also be a bit sceptical about such grandiose, sweeping statements as 'compassion and empathy' and 'trust and support'.

So I promise to explain it all in great detail. A little later.

Because first things first – the six prompts!

14 Yesterday's Best Thing (YBT)

1. Yesterday's Best Thing

2. Grateful For

3. Looking Forward To

4. Conscious Kindness

5. Compliment Sincerely

6. Greet Warmly

Probably the most compelling of the six prompts is 'Yesterday's Best Thing'.

In fact, when I start discussing IntheFlow with colleagues, friends and random strangers (as I do), YBT is the idea that they are all most enthusiastic and energised about.

The primary idea behind 'Yesterday's Best Thing' is the awakening of one's awareness 'muscle' by paying extraordinary attention to the ordinary things that are happening in your day.

Here's how it works:

Scan through your previous day. As you do so, keep a lookout for any experiences or feelings that made you feel good. These can relate to work or your personal life, and can be something obvious that jumps to mind instantly because of its stand-out quality, or something quite small that you need to search a little harder for.

Your only job as you go through this mental exercise is to recall what took place over the previous twenty-four hours, sifting through all the events, and then settling on the best moment of the day.

Essentially, what you are doing in this process is similar to a keyword search in your brain. Parts of our brain operate in the same way as a search engine, and depending on the 'keywords' we send in there, the mind obliges by focusing on experiences, emotions, sensations and thoughts containing the keyword.

Which in this case is 'best'.

So when you send your brain a message to look for the 'best' thing of the day, the internal conversation might go something like this: "Brain, we've got to look for the best thing that happened yesterday – let's recall what happened over the last twenty-four hours, and then make a decision on which of those was really great."

When I do this exercise, I sometimes feel like I'm making a little movie-style 'trailer package' of the day. And as I watch my personal montage, I point out selected events to myself, as if to say: "Look at that, wasn't that lovely? I didn't even notice it at the time."

Because it's almost always the case that with 'Yesterday's Best Thing', I become awake to some small, special moments that I had not given much attention or energy to at the time that they happened. It's only when I am prompted through 'YBT', that I become aware of them.

Sometimes, it may take a minute or so to finally settle on the event or experience that was the 'best', and as I do so, my internal dialogue says something like:

"Yes, that's the one."

For me, as I activate my attention and recall the events that took place the day before, I momentarily relive the experiences, which will sometimes evoke a smile or a sensation of warmth, almost like a little glow, as I recall something special.

Activated by paying focused attention, on purpose, mindfully.

But it's not just the really fantastic, stand-out moments of great days that gain attention with YBT. If you're doing the exercise every day (which of course you will), then invariably the average-to-somewhat-horrible days are included too.

And it's actually these more challenging days, when 'good-great-awesome' stuff is not obvious (or nowhere to be found at all), where I find real gratification – because by really looking hard, thinking back over twenty-four hours and scrutinising the details, I find my 'best' in some small, little experience – which would almost certainly have been passed over, totally unnoticed and unacknowledged.

A senior researcher at Jack Hammer told me this lovely story shortly after she joined our organisation and got into the rhythm of doing IntheFlow every morning:

> "By taking the time to focus on good and positive moments from a single day, you actually realise that every day is important and beautiful, and to appreciate the small stuff. When I was first asked what yesterday's best moment was, it literally opened a whole new train of thought. After being given the task to capture a best moment I realised 'WOW', yesterday wasn't just average ... it was fantastic. My daughter told me she loved me for the first time ..."

Which nearly made me cry with delight and joy that she had brought this precious moment into her awareness.

The reality is that without this type of directed exercise, a pretty average to middling day might pass by with no attention to its special (albeit quite ordinary) moments whatsoever.

What a pity.

Or worse – because we typically place a lot more time, energy and attention on frustrations, unhappiness and drama, a perfectly fine day with some quite lovely moments might get completely overshadowed by the negative events and emotions where we're dwelling.

And as for those absolutely disastrous days ... well, they usually don't stand a chance!

Ever hear yourself commenting that your day was just 'total chaos', or 'absolutely hectic', or 'completely awful'? Well, you might be tempted to believe yourself about how terrible, exhausting, stressful (add your typical drama words here) your life is.

Because what you pay attention to matters, remember?

When you're catastrophising like this, and using generalisation-style language, your mind will likely cloud and obscure any connection to the reality of your day. So you'll most likely miss out on the moments that are not totally, completely, absolutely horrible.

With the YBT prompt – a tiny, little, minute-long exercise – you achieve something considerable by encouraging yourself to pay attention in a different way, to moments that matter and stand out as 'best' regardless of how small or ordinary.

And 'best' is always possible to find, if you look for it.

As one of the Jack Hammer researchers so aptly commented:

> "I've noticed the impact of YBT mostly on my 'down' days – where searching for that one 'best' thing that happened to me yesterday creates a good feeling and essentially ups my mood."

Duly noted!

15 Grateful For (GF)

1. Yesterday's Best Thing

2. Grateful For

3. Looking Forward To

4. Conscious Kindness

5. Compliment Sincerely

6. Greet Warmly

Next up is a bit of gratitude and appreciation.

Yes, I accept, it can sound a little soppy and clichéd – I too have heard a million times about 'gratitude journals' and writing a list of ten things every day that one can be grateful for, just so that you have some perspective on how not-awful your life is ...

So I understand if you're reading this with a raised eyebrow.

However, if you're into hard-core science and data, there is an abundance of empirical evidence that validates the positive physical, emotional and psychological impact of cultivating an awareness of appreciation and thankfulness.

In *Thanks!* by Robert A. Emmons,[18] scientific research shows that regular thoughts of gratitude can improve one's sense of joy, optimism and happiness by about 25%, and *Gratitude Works!*[19] (by the same author who is a world expert in the field of 'gratitude science') offers a whole lot more data on the topic.

Even so, scientific evidence aside, you may still be feeling somewhat sceptical about dabbling in gratitude. So here's a direct instruction: Drop the raised eyebrow because IntheFlow's 'Grateful For' prompt has real impact.

Firstly, when I talk about gratitude, I'm not referring to things like the food I have to eat, the roof over my head, and such (although these are not to be taken for granted, of course).

Ideally, what I'm looking for is something more specific, something that relates to the happenings of the day, or the previous day. Something like, "I'm really grateful that my husband was able to take the children to school so that I could go to Pilates", or "I'm so grateful that I have an excellent dentist, who extracted my tooth relatively painlessly ..."

What I mean is that what we're 'Grateful For' is quite pedestrian, everyday stuff, that we often don't take note of or acknowledge, unless we actually think about it (like with Yesterday's Best Thing).

By focusing on the specifics of your day to identify something that you feel thankful and grateful for, you are once again bringing awareness to a few important moments of your day – things that are currently happening (or have already taken place) but which, until now, were not necessarily attracting much – or any – attention.

And with this mindful appreciation, comes a sense of enhanced empathy, generosity and compassion. And joy.

The science proves it, and I can confirm it!

Then, the 'Grateful For' prompt has a second part to it: once you've made a mental note of what you're 'grateful for', hold the thought and then take action.

Here's what I mean.

Hopefully, what you're feeling 'grateful for' involves another person – perhaps you're feeling thankful for or appreciative of something they've done, or how they 'show up' in your life. Because the opportunity then arises to make contact with that person to acknowledge them directly.

And this is the real power of the 'GF' prompt. It's all very well noting your gratitude in your mind, but when you pick up the phone and thank your husband, colleague, dentist, mother, whomever … that's when something extra special starts to happen.

I know this, because of the wonderful responses I get each and every time I say thank you unexpectedly to someone in my life.

And it is unexpected (which in a way makes it all the more special), because the reality is that even if we're particularly thoughtful and considerate people, and may think appreciatively of those around us, I'm pretty willing to bet that most of us do not take the extra step of actually saying 'thanks'.

Unless we make a point of doing it.

And with IntheFlow, that point is made. Every day.

When we shift our gratitude from thoughts into action, the person being thanked feels … well … appreciated. And acknowledged. And noticed. And loved. And … (I could go on here, but I know you get the point).

And you (the appreciator) will no doubt feel really good too.

The bottom line is that by focusing for a few moments on something that you're feeling grateful for in your life, and then taking a little extra time to act on this by acknowledging someone else, you create a circle of lovely energy and a consciousness of well-being.

All of which starts with just a few seconds of awareness.

16 Looking Forward To (LFT)

1. Yesterday's Best Thing

2. Grateful For

3. Looking Forward To

4. Conscious Kindness

5. Compliment Sincerely

6. Greet Warmly

Next up on the list is 'Looking Forward To'.

After the mental instruction to reflect and find 'Yesterday's Best Thing', then to think about something that I am feeling grateful for today, the next logical step in the mental 'geo-locating' is to project forward and scan the day ahead.

This is another way of bringing Mindful awareness and focus to the present – albeit with the intention of thinking not only about the present moment, but about the day as a whole.

The exercise activates an awareness of thoughts and feelings, and then (once again) shifts one into action mode.

Here's how it works:

Take a few seconds to scan the events of your day with the objective of identifying something that you feel – even a little – excited about as you think about that event or activity.

I usually do this while looking at my schedule in my calendar – sometimes a bit of a scary thing in itself, as my calendar is typically quite 'congested' – so that I can take in what lies ahead in an instant.

If you're fortunate enough to have something that immediately pops up as filling the criteria for 'Looking Forward To', that's great (and quite lucky). You'll know it's 'the one' when, as you think about it, you experience a sensation of 'glow', or feelings of contentedness, excitement or anticipation. Perhaps a glimmer of a smile.

The conversation in your head might go something like 'Can't wait for that', or 'That's going to be fun/enjoyable/relaxing ... etc'.

But if nothing 'pops', don't stress!

Because in reality, most days are not wildly exciting, invigorating or inspiring. There's usually a regularity and structure to our days which – frankly – is necessary to cope with all the moving parts of our lives.

I know that a lot of the time, I'd be quite delighted with a bit of predictability and steadiness.

So, to be clear, with 'Looking Forward To', the intention is not to try to find, or to expect, something overtly spectacular that miraculously appears in your schedule. Instead, the 'Looking Forward To' (LFT) prompt is intended to help us pay attention to the moments of our day in a different way. To notice their special quality, how they make us feel, and how that impacts our perception of the day.

In addition, what prompt number three, 'LFT' offers is a 'beacon of light' to keep your eye on when things get a little (or a lot) dull, chaotic or stressful during the course of the day. Something to focus on when the inevitable curve-balls of the day begin their trajectory towards you.

Have you noticed that days sometimes (well, more than sometimes to be honest) have a way of meandering downhill even after the most promising of starts? I often find that my day starts out great – possibly it's the after-glow of a morning meditation session, or a general state of greater energy in the morning (possibly my double shot of caffeine) – and therefore with greater robustness to the little pieces of shrapnel that start heading my way.

By later on in the day, many of my best intentions have faded – and this is when my 'LFT' really comes in handy. Something to look forward to! That really helps when the going gets tough.

Because let's face it – when it comes to the day-to-day-ness of every single job on earth, there are none that are consistently fabulous, stimulating and exciting.

In fact, most jobs (and I know this because I run an executive search firm, remember, and I've spoken to thousands of people in thousands of different roles over the years) have some element of not-particularly-interesting.

Nevertheless, routine should not equate to monotony, flatness or boredom. Structure should not result in a lack of spontaneity or rule out the daily inclusion of something lovely and fun that we can look forward to – particularly on tough days.

So imagine you've arrived at work and today is one of those nothing-much-happening days. What 'LFT' does for you is it directs you to think about your day up ahead and to find ONE thing that stands out as something enjoyable, interesting or special. As your mind settles on it, you might experience a thought that goes 'Yes, that's going to be cool, fun, (replace with your own word).'

The thing is, our days often already include an element of 'Looking Forward To' – but we've just not paid it any special attention, or thought about the event or activity in this way.

And it's such a simple thing: to direct one's mind, deliberately and on purpose, to focus (almost like a spotlight) on something small and possibly quite ordinary, which – purely with the energy of your attention – can help you to be present to the 'journey' of your day. (Here's a Mindfulness-based idea again, in case you missed it!)

Now, I must contend that some days present neither overt nor semi-concealed moments to look forward to, at all! There are those days that feel like obstacle courses that need deft navigation just to emerge unscathed, and then there are those that are filled with anxiety and trepidation:

The meeting with your boss.

The conversation with your child's teacher.

The dinner with your spouse's colleagues.

The networking event where you don't know ANYONE.

This list could go on and on. And On. But let's stop here. I'm sure you know what I'm referring to.

Well, 'Looking Forward To' can really help on days like these. Because if, after having done your mental scan of the day up ahead you cannot find one single thing that's making you go "aha, I'm looking forward to THAT", then you need to take action and plan something that you can fit into your day that will generate the 'looking forward to' feeling.

It could be anything at all – a walk around your block when you get home, a bath with candles, making a special dinner, calling a friend for a chat – ANYTHING that works for you.

I have found my entire day turn around when I have focused on the LFT prompt.

Most of my life consists of juggling a thousand balls (so I can hardly call my days boring or lacking variety), but of course I have those days where none of the balls are particularly fun or interesting. They're the same balls I juggled yesterday, and they'll be the same balls I will have to keep in the air tomorrow.

Which has its own monotony.

So on those days when I do the forward scan, and I can't find a single event, meeting or even non-work activity to hang my 'Looking Forward To' hat on, I make a plan to change that.

As a result, I frequently find myself thinking up some really lovely ideas to shake up the day. A beach walk, meeting a friend for a quick coffee, buying an ice cream and eating it for ten minutes on the promenade, taking a fifteen-minute meander through the city centre where I work, a special craft activity with my children, listening to a podcast on the way home – the list is endless.

And, as you can see, not particularly special in an extraordinary, 'out-there' way. In fact, quite the opposite – these are all quite ordinary, inexpensive, non-time-consuming experiences. Yet, by focusing, selecting and deciding to make time for them, they take on a specialness.

For me, this is the perfect way to remind myself to enjoy the 'journey' of my day, instead of rushing to the end destination.

It is of course tempting to say, 'My day is so hectic, I have not got one extra second to schedule in one more thing.'

But the point is – if your day is so busy, but within that there is not one single thing that you're actually looking forward to doing, then you're in trouble. It is then even MORE essential to squeeze in something that will potentially change the way you feel about your whole day, even if it lasts for fifteen minutes.

So, with 'LFT', think about your day and find something to look forward to. And if nothing 'looking-forward-to-ish' comes to mind, you need to think a little harder to find something that you're going to do today that you WILL look forward to.

Then, schedule it into your calendar, and just do it. It is highly likely that your 'LFT' today is going to be your 'YBT' tomorrow!

17 Conscious Kindness (CK)

1. Yesterday's Best Thing

2. Grateful For

3. Looking Forward To

4. Conscious Kindness

5. Compliment Sincerely

6. Greet Warmly

When the Jack Hammer team initially started with our IntheFlow practice, we called this prompt 'Random Act of Kindness', which I had borrowed from Shawn Achor's TED Talk 'The happy secret to better work'.[20] In the talk, he lists several factors contributing to a sense of happiness, one of them being a 'Random Act of Kindness', the objective of which is to randomly and opportunistically do something nice or kind for someone else.

It sounded like a great idea.

Because the sad reality is that in this busy life of ours, when it is sometimes a battle just to get through the day, we seldom look up and out at what's going on in our very near surroundings. There's just no time or energy for anything other than keeping our heads down and pushing through.

Or at least that's what we tell ourselves.

And as a result, we infrequently reach out to the people around us (family, friends, work colleagues, acquaintances, strangers) and do something special, something kind, something thoughtful, that is unexpected, not asked for, and with no expectation of anything in return.

This last point is quite important. Ask yourself this question: How often do you do nice, thoughtful, kind things for another with no 'agenda' (a caveat to this might be spouse and kids, when you're in a particularly good mood)?

Don't blush if the answer you find is "Ummh ... infrequently".

You're not alone.

We live in a world of 'I scratch your back, you scratch mine'. If I do something for you, 'you owe me one'.

When we put ourselves out there, or 'go beyond the call of duty' for another, there is typically an implicit expectation of reciprocity. At times, we are even more deliberate or calculating in our actions, in that the motivation for doing something kind for another is the hope or desire for a reciprocal favour.

So the idea of a random act of kindness – in particular one with no strings attached – struck me as an opportunity to positively impact the life of someone else, even briefly. I loved the idea of doing something thoughtful, even a really small thing, for someone else, in an agenda-less way.

I was further inspired by a story I call 'Lady-Walking-Dog', where I witnessed a beautifully random act of kindness as I was driving home one windy evening.

As I sat waiting for the light to change, I caught sight of a woman walking her dog along the road.

I'm not sure if the sight was entirely arbitrary, or if there was something special about this person with her hair flying in the wind (perhaps I was thinking about how glad I was not to have to do a chore like this on a windy Cape Town day), but there was clearly something quite unique and wonderful about this woman, as became evident a few seconds later.

I had probably been texting on my phone, which I tend to do when waiting at traffic lights (my bad!), and when I looked up again, I caught sight of her holding the arm of a blind man with a walking cane. It seemed that he had gone off course and was heading towards an alley before 'Lady-Walking-Dog' retrieved him from the alley and helped him on his way. They crossed the road together, and once he was safely back on track, she continued on her dog-walking task.

I recall feeling an odd sensation in my body as I watched this – warmth, and a tightness in my throat that usually precedes tears of happiness (I know this, because it happens every time I watch a movie where the underdog wins the race, or hearing about firemen rescuing people, etc).

And then flooding thoughts about how our lives could all be experienced in such a different way if people were even a *little* kinder to one another.

I instantly wanted to be 'Lady-Walking-Dog' – kinder, a little less self-involved, a lot more empathetic and compassionate.

So 'Random Act of Kindness' became a key element of IntheFlow.

I had initially thought that opportunities for kindness and generosity would present themselves in abundance, and it would merely be a matter of grabbing one of these many chances which would appear 'randomly', and acting on it.

After many days in a row of not coming anywhere close to fulfilling this element of IntheFlow, I realised that this one was going to take more effort than keeping a beady eye open and hoping for some 'Lady-Waking-Dog' opportunity to magically appear before me.

In fact, if just left to random chance, I was likely to not do a single 'random act of kindness' all week.

And the Jack Hammer team was equally frustrated. One of my Jack Hammer colleagues, after a week of 'blanking' on this, threw her hands up in despair claiming, "There is nothing random about this at all!"

I realised that this element of IntheFlow needed a tweak. The opportunities don't just miraculously appear. They need to be deliberately and consciously sought out, and sometimes even pre-arranged.

So we decided to change 'Random Act of Kindness' to 'Conscious Kindness'.

Which is undoubtedly the most challenging of the six prompts to execute consistently because it requires much more deliberate thought and action.

But perhaps because it is a little harder to execute than the others, it is also one of the most powerful and impactful of the six. Certainly, the great feelings that arise when I perform an act of 'Conscious Kindness' are worth the extra effort.

Just think about how it must feel to have someone do something kind, something considerate, something thoughtful for you, which is also completely unexpected and comes with no obligation for you to do anything in return.

How would you feel?

I'll speak for myself and say that receiving an unexpected, no-strings-attached kindness like this makes me feel simply happy. And content. And warm inside. And restored. And fulfilled (after I've recovered from the surprise of it).

And as the giver, the impact is even greater.

Because the thing about kindness is that the mere act itself is so powerful that it has an equal or even more powerful impact on the giver than the recipient.

I guess that if you're a particularly sceptical sceptic, you might argue that doing an act of Conscious Kindness, with the objective of feeling great yourself is not an entirely agenda-less act. Which is probably true, but I'm totally OK with that.

Knock yourself out with acts of Conscious Kindness if it makes you feel good! That's what's supposed to happen.

On some days, I must admit, the act of kindness is no more than an extra tip for a car guard[2] or waiter. And then there are days when I do things out of a sense of obligation, knowing that it was the 'right thing to do', but not feeling particularly compassionate or kind in my heart.

Interestingly, on all of these occasions, regardless of intent or motivation, I have found myself feeling very glad at having acted. What was initially an obligatory act lacking in 'proper' empathy, turned into feelings of real fulfilment and happiness.

I'm sure, too, that in all of these instances, no matter how small, I received as much – if not more – from my acts of kindness, than the recipients themselves.

But the best acts of Conscious Kindness are the ones that are a little more planned and require more than a passing thought.

Recently, I heard that one of the Jack Hammer researchers had sent a gift of flowers to her colleague, who works remotely in another city, because she'd become aware that the 'remoter' was feeling particularly miserable due to her husband embarking on a two-month business trip.

Naturally, the remoter was blown away at the gesture!

---

2   Car guard: A car guard is an informally employed person in charge of finding parking spots for cars and ensuring the safety of those cars until their owners return. These self-employed individuals often charge a nominal fee. This occurs most often in South African cities. https://en.wikipedia.org/wiki/Car_guard

On a daily basis, I find Jack Hammer staff members going out of their way to be supportive, generous and considerate to their peers, as well as to people in their respective communities – neighbours, charitable institutions, as well as random people in need.

Not to say that they wouldn't ordinarily act in such a way – but undoubtedly, a special focus on 'CK', even periodically, helps one to 'go the extra mile'.

Interestingly, despite the earlier statement that the best acts of Conscious Kindness are the planned ones, what has also dawned on me over time is that *being* 'consciously kind' may suffice – without the kindness necessarily being overtly evidenced in *actions* towards others.

Let me elaborate: stopping for a few moments to become aware of one's state (thoughts, emotions, sensations), and accepting that current state without being critical or judgemental of oneself, is simple and pure kindness. To oneself.

The internal dialogue, instead of the 'snap out of it' or 'get a grip' or 'stop being a @#$%' variety, would go like this: 'ok, so this is how it is right now.' This Mindfulness-based approach – to 'meet oneself where one's at' – is a true act of kindness and compassion.

And if one can cultivate 'conscious kindness' in this way for oneself, the possibilities towards others are well within reach, without necessarily doing anything grandiose at all.

When we practise 'Conscious Kindness' we're practising Mindfulness: Firstly, it requires deliberate present-moment attention and focus. Secondly, it provides an opportunity – in a very practical way – to develop and experience compassion, empathy and loving kindness. To others, and to oneself.

18 Compliment Sincerely (CS)

1. Yesterday's Best Thing

2. Grateful For

3. Looking Forward To

4. Conscious Kindness

5. Compliment Sincerely

6. Greet Warmly

'Compliment Sincerely' has some similarities to 'Conscious Kindness' – it also requires you to be opportunistic in looking out for the chance to offer a compliment to someone else, in a way that is unexpected, unasked for, and with no expectation of reciprocation.

The story behind 'Compliment Sincerely' comes from a shopping experience whilst on holiday in California. I was trying on a jacket in a store, when all of a sudden a woman next to me said, "You look great in that."

Upon hearing this unsolicited compliment, my instinctive internal response was, "Oh, that's very nice", followed almost immediately by, "She must be a sales person employed by the store."

Because why on earth would a complete stranger randomly pay me such a lovely, unexpected compliment, if there wasn't some additional motivation or agenda for her to say such a thing?

That someone could just say something like that without an ulterior motive only dawned on me a few seconds later, when I realised that she was just another customer. Paying me a sincere and genuine compliment.

My feeling after that was a flood of warmth and delight. And of course, I bought the jacket (which DOES look great on me, by the way).

The jacket that inspired 'Compliment Sincerely'.
It still attracts compliments, particularly from my
daughters who adore the feel of the fabric when
they hug me. (Photo by Hetty Zantman)

This experience prompted some thinking.

What I realised was that there are many occasions when I have very positive, flattering and complimentary thoughts about others, but I seldom take the further step of articulating this to them.

"Why not?" I asked myself.

And 'myself' answered: "The reality of the world in the urban jungle, which many of us occupy, is that we're too busy, or too pre-occupied, or too self-involved, or too distracted, or too worried about what others might think, or too scared of looking stupid, or too something-or-another to shift a complimentary thought from its comfortable, safe spot in our minds to an articulated sentence directed to another."

In other words, we don't take the extra step of complimenting others ... for no particularly good reason at all!

I also decided that the benefits of doing this act far outweighed the lame excuses for not doing it, and so 'Compliment Sincerely' was incorporated into IntheFlow.

This meant that on a daily basis, I started noticing when my brain was offering a mental compliment to someone (the Mindfulness bit), and then I would deliberately act on this by articulating the thought, in audible words, to the individual concerned.

I can't deny it: the first few times I tried this out, I had some 'gulp' moments. And so I totally understand that for someone who is a little shy or introverted this may feel like an impossible task.

But if you can gather the courage to transfer the compliment from inside your head to the person who deserves it ... oh WOW, the impact of this little act is fantastic!

The recipient will no doubt experience positive emotions of some sort, but – even better – you will most likely feel pretty good too.

The only requirement being that the compliment needs to be sincere and genuine. Easy enough!

Now, I have realised over time that it doesn't really matter too much whether the response from the 'complimentee' (that's a made-up word, I think) is hugely effusive and expressive, or somewhere between ambivalent and non-existent (although of course it's undeniably lovely to have a positive reaction to one's acknowledgement).

For me, the pleasure is in the noticing and in the 'gifting' to another. This also means that I don't rely on the feedback of the recipient as a measure of whether my compliment was 'good enough', and so there is no self-judgement attached to this.

Now, as with all of the other elements of IntheFlow, there are days when it seems that absolutely no complimenting opportunities present themselves. It's on these days that a little bit of focused attention will almost always yield great outcomes.

I vividly recall one evening when, despite my good intentions to compliment some deserving person during the course of the day, no one had yet been the recipient of my flattery. I decided to focus my attention with more diligence, and within minutes of my effort, the opportunity presented itself beautifully.

My husband and I were out that evening, and were passing by Cape Town's Eastern Bazaar for a quick Indian meal. Behind the counter, I noticed the cashier wearing a very pretty blouse – probably because the white shirt, made from a silky fabric, was quite out of place, considering the restaurant's canteen style and risk of curry stains.

As soon as the thought came to my mind ('that's a pretty blouse'), I grabbed it and decided to translate my thought into a sincere compliment to the cashier –

who was completely taken aback. She looked at me as if I was totally daft, and said nothing.

I could just as easily have moved on, pretending that the compliment-issuing episode had not happened, but I really wanted to make sure that she'd heard me. So I felt compelled to repeat myself. "That's a lovely blouse," I said again, a little louder. Which on this occasion was met with a genuine smile.

Reward enough for me.

Over time, 'CS' has become one of the easier-to-execute elements of IntheFlow – more often than not, I spontaneously articulate the complimentary thoughts roaming around in my brain to the people around me.

And I keep wondering why I waited so long to begin this practice. It takes almost no effort or time, and the buzzy, glowing energy that surrounds this action between the giver and the receiver is just, well, lovely.

Give this a shot. It will be interesting to see what happens when you stop, break your usual patterns, and try out something new.

19 Greet Warmly (GW)

1. Yesterday's Best Thing

2. Grateful For

3. Looking Forward To

4. Conscious Kindness

5. Compliment Sincerely

6. Greet Warmly

So finally – 'Greet Warmly'.

This is the last of the six daily prompts that make up IntheFlow – other than the 'alternate' prompts that you can interchange, or add to the six, when things start to get stale or need some shaking up (more about that in an upcoming chapter).

Now, a warm greeting doesn't sound like anything particularly special. And frankly, it's not. But considering that at the time I was developing the IntheFlow practice, I was spending my life with my eyes cast down, and very closed off from the people in my immediate surroundings, engaging at all (never mind warmly) with others required conscious effort.

Because I was so intensely focused inwards, holding myself together to just get through the day whilst performing my wild juggling act, my attitude in general was one of 'don't talk to me, don't bother me, don't engage with me ... because I'm busy'.

Not with my family, friends and work colleagues, of course (well, sometimes with them too ...), but mostly with anyone else I would encounter. Cashiers, delivery-men, neighbours, the sort-of strangers at the coffee shop whom I see every day because they're regulars like me, but I've never stopped to say hello or even smile ... acquaintances that I've seen 'around' but would not have paused to engage with because ...

Why?

Well, because it would take too much of my time and energy!

And this is when I looked at myself and realised that this internal dialogue was becoming pretty ridiculous.

Too busy and too tired to say hello and offer a smile?

Granted, there was a fair amount of self-judgement going on here, but there are times when a bit of a 'wake-up-and-get-real' is needed.

And so I decided to try something different. To change the aspect of my line of sight, to gaze upward and outward, to look the random strangers (or familiar acquaintances) in the eye and offer a warm greeting. With a smile.

So let's just consider the science of smiling for a moment.

Once again, if we're looking for scientifically proven evidence, there is a tremendous amount of research on the science of smiling – including the impact that smiling has on your emotional state, on customer-service experience, on work-related happiness ... well, the list is pretty long.

In a wonderful TED talk entitled 'The Hidden Power of Smiling' Ron Gutman summarises a whole range of studies which show that smiling can predict longevity and overall well-being, as well as reduce stress, increase endorphin levels and lower blood pressure.[21]

And I know for sure in my daily work that when I'm on the phone with candidates or clients, if I smile during my conversation, extra energy is created. It carries through to my voice, and the outcomes of the 'smiling' calls versus the non-smiling ones are far more impactful.

'Greet Warmly' combines attention, action and emotional connection. So simple. NO real effort at all. But it does require you to come off autopilot, to stop for a minute, to be present to the here and now, and to engage mindfully with another. Just for a moment.

Meaning that the passing, half-attentive, not-really-present, somewhat distracted, multi-tasking style of greeting does not qualify!

Hello and a smile ... which sometimes leads to a bit of a chat which might hold one up for an extra minute or two. But worth it. Because when you offer a warm greeting to someone, they will automatically and inevitably do the same for you (aside from the cold fish people, like I used to be!).

And this human exchange of warm positive energy makes all parties to the interaction feel, well, quite nice. At the very least.

After a presentation of IntheFlow to a group of entrepreneurs, I received many emails from them, telling me how IntheFlow had impacted them, their lives, their work, and their general state of consciousness and happiness.

The most surprising and heart-warming of these messages was from the very successful founder and CEO of a national training organisation. He said to me that he loved IntheFlow, but of all the rituals, was getting the biggest kick out of 'Greet Warmly'. He hadn't realised how aloof he had become, how abrupt and closed off from the people around him until he started making a conscious effort to 'greet warmly'. And the immediate impact was amazing. He couldn't believe how an action which took such little effort could give back such a great reward.

Scientific research aside, both you and I know from experience that it's hard to be miserable or angry concurrent with the act of smiling. Even if you're in the worst, blackest, darkest mood, smiling and greeting will almost ALWAYS (and I'm willing to guarantee this, or give you your money back) shift a cloudy mood to something a little lighter, at least.

And all it takes is a small act of Mindfulness – becoming aware of one's present state, and making a conscious and deliberate decision to shift one's energy, to engage with others.

20 Write it down

So there you have it. The six prompts of IntheFlow.

Pretty simple, right? Not rocket science, right? Easy to just get going and do it, right?

'Yes!' I hear you shout with a resounding bellow.

I'm hoping that you can't wait to get started. But before you do, there are a few more things to discuss in order to maximise the impact of IntheFlow and achieve the benefits I alluded to earlier.

So keep reading – we're not done yet.

First up: writing.

Having read many, many books and articles on goal-setting (and listened to as many audio-books and podcasts, as well as great conference speakers, on the topic), there is one aspect of the goal-setting process that everyone agrees with. There is probably even some scientific research to prove this point.

Which is: 'Write it down!'

Because it's one thing to think a thought. That's a good start, particularly if it's a good thought.

But for a thought to gain some traction, momentum or 'stickiness', writing it out is the answer. The action of writing is a commitment, it makes ideas visible and present, and in this way further brings one's thoughts and feelings into awareness.

I know for myself that I can do the mental gymnastics part very easily: 'What was yesterday's best thing? What is my GF? What am I looking forward to today?' etc. A few seconds, a bit of thinking and mental scanning, and boom, IntheFlow is done. Tick.

A good start, but not as much power or impact as might be achieved by taking another minute or two to pen those thoughts.

So, for IntheFlow, I've borrowed from all of the goal-setting literature I've ever read, and included a 'write it down' component.

By taking the extra time (still very quick, mind you) with the writing activity, one naturally applies additional focus and attention. And it's a great way to compel ourselves to stop, wake up from autopilot and become aware of the present via the six prompts.

When I initially introduced IntheFlow to my team, I provided each of them with a laminated 'Prompt Card', with the acronyms of the six daily prompts listed on the left of the card, and space to write next to it.

≡the FLOW

1. **YBT** (Yesterday's Best Thing) ....

2. **GF** (Grateful For)..

3. **LFT** (Looking Forward To)...

4. **RAK** (Random Act of Kindness).......................................

5. **GW** (Greet Warmly) ....

6. **CS** (Compliment Sincerely)...

This is the prompt card we use at Jack Hammer. I use it like a whiteboard, writing and erasing each day. Any print shop can make one for you, using laminated hard plastic. Wipe with a cloth, or erase with a pencil eraser.

The card is a 6cm x 20cm piece of laminated cardboard (very inexpensive), which almost any print shop will be able to make for you.

The reason for laminating the card is to enable one to write on it with a whiteboard marker and then erase each day. The card has proved very durable – written on each day with a marker and erased with a standard pencil eraser or cloth.

I then stick the card with some Prestik on my computer monitor, where I can see it all day. You could also place the card on the wall in front of you, on window surfaces, or some other visible spot.

It's quite nice to have your IntheFlow notes positioned in this way – as opposed to tucked away in the pages of a notebook. I like referring to my prompt card during the day, particularly to remind myself about 'Looking Forward To', as well as to fill any empty spaces for the likes of 'CS', 'GW' or 'CK'.

I practise my 'personal' IntheFlow exercise by writing out my thoughts on the prompt card. I like to keep it visible, so I stick it on my monitor with Prestik. Not elegant, but very practical.

But you can use pretty much anything that works for you – a notebook, a piece of scrap paper or a digital device.

There are certainly days when I feel so busy that my internal dialogue goes something like this: "OK, I've thought about my YBT, GF, LFT, got it, great, move on."

But I know I'm short-changing myself by not taking the extra step of writing it down. There's something quite 'airy' about thoughts, versus the much more 'solid', committed action of writing words onto paper (or whatever platform you choose).

And if you're looking to train your awareness muscle, writing (much like breathing) is a great anchor for this.

So, here's the instruction: Write it down!

PART 2

TRANSFORMING TEAM CULTURE

21 Sharing is caring

We've now reached the part of the book where we start heading into the 'transforming team culture' bit. This has been alluded to in the introductory chapters – but until now we've been focusing on the personal self-awareness aspect of IntheFlow.

When I initially developed IntheFlow, it was intended purely to develop and support my own self-awareness, and to help cultivate an awareness of the ordinary (yet special) moments of my day that I was not paying any attention to. I had wanted to connect with the present (the journey) instead of being fixated on goals and outcomes (the destination), as I had begun to realise that I was 'arriving' feeling empty inside.

And IntheFlow really worked for me. Quickly.

So I couldn't wait to share the delight and excitement that I was experiencing using the six prompts with my team at Jack Hammer.

A quick sidebar about the wonderful people I have the great fortune to work with every day. Firstly, I refer to them as my 'work friends', a perfectly apt phrase coined by my children, and an accurate way of articulating the deep respect and love that I have for the exceptional people who work at Jack Hammer. Secondly, they have over the years become very accustomed to me arriving at work with some 'creative' idea or another.

So when I described IntheFlow to them, and asked them if they wanted to give it a shot, they jumped right in with a unanimous 'Yes'.

Initially, it was a big experiment. I had absolutely no idea of what the impact would be, although my hoped-for outcomes were mostly around increasing productivity by virtue of each staff member experiencing enhanced self-awareness and connection with the special moments of their lives.

What transpired as we went through the process was a most unexpected – and magnificent – surprise. And the 'surprise' – **a substantial and significant shift in team and company culture** – happened because of the *sharing* element of IntheFlow.

I cannot articulate the impact better than the individuals who experienced this.

Here's part of a note I received from one of the junior researchers in the team. Despite being in her mid-20s at the time of writing, the maturity of her comments belie her age:

> "There is an enhanced sense of personal commitment to the team, because they are no longer just people you work with. Their life priorities are clear to you from being a witness to the aspects of their lives that excite them most. This enhanced commitment makes for a happier place where you feel your worth exceeds a professional function, aiding and enhancing professional performance."

I was blown away by this feedback when I first received it. Pretty profound! I knew that shifts were taking place, but to see it articulated like this was very affirming.

Over time, I received additional insights into the impact of IntheFlow on relationships within the team:

"Sharing one's moments and thoughts with one another brings out a certain vulnerability which has the effect of bringing one closer to one's team mates. I would now climb the highest mountain for a team mate because I've gotten to know them at a deeper level! And the team is the company, isn't it?"

"IntheFlow has resulted in a much deeper understanding of the people I work with. This is such an awesome way to discover what truly motivates members of the team, in a way that is playful and habit-forming."

"IntheFlow helps us to work together with more consideration for one another. It builds mutual respect, consciousness of each other's differences and, more importantly, a reinforcement of the many things we share despite our different ages, cultures, races and personal situations."

Now, we all know that cohesive teams made up of people who trust and respect one another, and are therefore happier and less stressed in their work environments are also optimally productive.

So, in a round-about way, the initial intention of enhanced productivity was fulfilled through IntheFlow.

But this turned out to be just the tip of the iceberg.

Because what we also gained was compassion. And empathy. And understanding. And trust. Together, through IntheFlow, we co-created a culture of insight, wisdom and compassion.

22 Exactly HOW does IntheFlow impact team culture?

Yes, I know that a business environment of compassion and trust may sound a little far-fetched.

Particularly if you're working in one of those somewhat toxic (or even moderately unpleasant) work environments.

However, even if you're lucky enough to enjoy working with your colleagues and to feel respect for (and respected by) your boss, it's seldom that team relationships are described as supportive, trusting, nourishing and compassionate.

Now, before we started practising IntheFlow, the culture at Jack Hammer was pretty good (or so I've been told). But I doubt anyone would have used those kinds of descriptors to account for the work environment.

It's only when we started practising IntheFlow daily that the big transformation started to happen. And it only happens if the group of people are willing to share – even a little – about what they think, feel and notice.

Simple as that.

IntheFlow impacts and transforms team culture when people share, authentically, a little bit about themselves every day.

Excepting that for some people, the idea of sharing anything authentically personal or emotionally revealing about themselves with anyone (let alone work colleagues) may sound like an absolutely terrible idea. Awful, horrible, #nothappening!

And that's understandable. It can be pretty scary to share personal stuff. It can make one feel quite (or very) vulnerable, particularly if you've never tried this before. And particularly where trust is lacking in one's team or group of colleagues.

So if you've decided that now's the time to call it quits with IntheFlow – nice ideas, but this sharing bit is so 'not happening' – don't be overly hasty in making that decision (and after all, you've read a LOT already, so hang in there …).

Firstly, let's not get overly psychologically analytical about this. As with all of the other aspects of IntheFlow, the sharing bit is just as practical and uncomplicated.

Here's how it works:

Each team member emails their 'YBT' to one team member (in our case, it's the office manager), who consolidates all the emails into one, and then around mid-morning sends out one email to the whole team, which we call our 'IntheFlow Report'.

Every single day of the work week. Without fail.

The IntheFlow Report takes the form of a bullet-point email, with each team member's 'YBT' (and one other element – to be discussed later), in which each person has offered their colleagues a little snapshot of what's going on in their lives.

And it's often stuff outside of the work context – big and small highlights (as well as sometimes some lowlights) – that we share about ourselves, and that would probably not be part of general conversation while you're making a cup of tea in the kitchen or standing outside for a smoke.

Sometimes light and superficial, sometimes pretty deep and meaningful, the IntheFlow Report provides a unique window – or fresh perspective – to one another's lives, that we would not otherwise have access to.

I have been brought to tears on occasion – tears of laughter, as well as tears of gratitude, pride, delight, compassion, sadness (the full suite of emotions, in fact) – when reading my daily email.

Here are a few little 'stories' that have come out of the IntheFlow Report, that I am absolutely certain I would never have heard without this platform:

> 'I played the "pregnancy card" to cut the queue at Nando's! Listen, the line was about 20 people long, and I was desperate for spicy food – my appetite has kicked into overdrive. I eyed a lady behind the counter and dashed over and said, "I'm really sorry but I'm heavily pregnant and can't stand in such a long queue." She was very polite and took my order without any questions!'

> 'As a young girl growing up I never ever had a boyfriend. I was that girl that was never interested or just too shy about it. Then this beautiful guy came into my life. He was my forever after, the love of my life – but as life would have it our paths separated. It is with a very sad heart that I was told of his untimely demise last night – all of 47 years! It is so sad that we never had the chance to say goodbye. Life is so precious – just hold on and love and live every minute as nothing is guaranteed.'

> 'My horrible little car (which I can't help but love) has to be one of the few models on the road that'll get you to work and back with a broken radiator (with a bit of a "screwdriver and bucket" fix in between) and

then cost you just a few Rand for a brand new radiator, installed and ready to go within an hour ...'

⁙

'Last night I let my mother know that we won't be spending Christmas Day with her. If that doesn't sound brave, then your mother and mine are very different!!!'

⁙

'Mmmmm ... so nothing worked out as planned yesterday. Internet down at the office, went home to work from there and my home laptop had given up after 4 years so had to go buy a new home computer and install software and wait for folders to sync from the cloud ... overall just a horrible day. What was good in all of this? The fact that I had the means to go out and buy another computer without worrying that I can't afford it; the fact that I had a lovely couch to fall asleep on; the fact that I love my home and totally dig the people I work with. So YBT – the Universe reminding me that Gratitude changes your Attitude.'

Over time, each team member has gained trust in the process, and has been willing to share quite personal information, allowing themselves to be a little (or a lot) vulnerable among their peers. **And this is how the compassion, the understanding, the support, trust, respect and love has developed in the team.**

When I first introduced the idea of the IntheFlow Report, there may have been some scepticism from the team, around whether there was an ulterior motive or agenda to the exercise. Frankly, if any team leader introduces this to a group where there IS an agenda, it will never work, and certainly never achieve the tremendous team culture gains that we experienced at Jack Hammer.

The sharing of IntheFlow is never intended as 'ammunition' to be 'used' against anyone. It is not a 'management tool'. There is no 'agenda', beyond genuine, authentic connection.

In addition, there's a 'safety net' with the sharing, in that no one is ever required or compelled to share more than they're comfortable with. And over time, as each member of the group feels more and more comfortable, and safer with the process, they are likely to take greater risks in what they share with the team.

I've seen this in action at Jack Hammer – where for quite a few YEARS, one of our colleagues only shared information about what meal had been cooked, prepared or eaten the previous day. It took ages for trust to build and for her to share anything more personal than that.

Of course, there are the 'over-sharers' in any group – and they usually plunge in, enabling the others to feel comfortable with the experience.

And when the whole group is at ease with one another, it makes it really simple for new team members to settle right in.

When newbies join Jack Hammer, we introduce IntheFlow as part of the onboarding process. Fortunately, our screening for 'fit' is mostly quite accurate (well, it should be – we're executive search specialists and interview people for a living!), so we have never had a new recruit say 'no way, you guys are loony if you think I'm playing this game'.

Even so, I don't underestimate how challenging and foreign it may be for people who come from uptight, hierarchical, gossipy work environments to go with IntheFlow. But once they see everyone from the CEO to the receptionist engaging in an open, authentic manner, they soon get over any concerns or squeamishness.

For some encouragement, here's what one of my more 'conservative' staff members had to say about this:

> "The biggest impact, and possibly the most important thing IntheFlow has taught me is to 'share' – to appreciate, to compliment, to express – without any expectation or design of a response."

And without a doubt, by using IntheFlow as a team communication tool, companies have the opportunity to transform and shift the culture of a team to the next level.

23 Making it work – it doesn't happen by itself

So here comes the instruction manual, the nuts and bolts, the logistics of making this whole thing work.

And which is as important as the content itself.

As previously mentioned, I love reading books, listening to podcasts and attending conferences which centre around personal and leadership development, motivation and goal-setting, the world of work, the organisational culture ... (well, actually the list is quite long).

I fit the typical 'entrepreneur' stereotype in that I adore new ideas and I write copious notes, filling many, many notebooks with my tiny, neat, pencilled handwriting (I still prefer this to digital note-taking).

And I am almost always inspired (even a little) by the ideas and knowledge presented by the author or speaker, who are typically passionate experts on the topic at hand.

But the inspiration sadly doesn't last very long – and most often, I don't act on the great concepts because I have no SYSTEM to transition the ideas from my notebook into something that can have a meaningful, sustainable impact.

So although it's lovely to just enjoy hearing or reading new content, which can enlighten, educate, and provoke thoughts and insights, what a pity if the opportunity to use the content is missed.

Now, not all content requires action, nor is all content worthy of implementation or further engagement – but for the nuggets that arise from time to time, where one instantly thinks, "Great idea, I could use this in X, Y or Z way"... without a system or a plan of some sort to incorporate the idea in a practical manner into your day, the likelihood of the 'nugget' heading to the Graveyard of Great Ideas is high.

Shamefully, my beautiful, neat notebooks have become massive pits of death for many great ideas that never saw the light of day because I didn't have an easy system to transition the ideas into practice.

And I really do NOT want that to happen with the concepts and ideas you have read about here.

So (together with my team), I've developed a system, to enable the use of IntheFlow as a communication tool in your team.

There's a big BUT, though:

For IntheFlow to become something more than a great idea you read in this book, it is going to require practice and discipline.

Which all starts sounding a little (or a lot) dreary and off-putting. However, if you recall, earlier in the book, I promised that the practice part of IntheFlow is really simple.

In fact, my specific words were: 'incredibly simple to understand, truly easy – and enjoyable – to execute, and very well-supported with cues and reminders'.

And I'll make good on this promise.

24 Four easy steps

So here's the system to make it work.

In four easy steps:

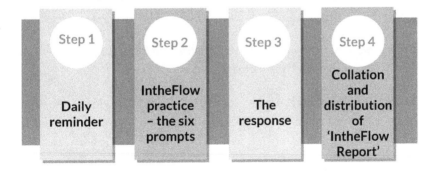

OK, let's elaborate.

Step 1: Daily reminder

This is critical, and despite hundreds and hundreds of days of practising IntheFlow, I still need my cue. At Jack Hammer this comes in the form of an email, sent to the entire team at 8.00 am by our office administrator (who is also the one who collates and distributes the IntheFlow Report in Step 4).

The email is intended to remind everyone to practise their own personal IntheFlow exercise (the six prompts – think, write, act), and to respond.

I realised how important this trigger was when our administrator went on leave for two weeks and one of the other team members stepped in to manage the IntheFlow Report.

The 'stand-in' reminded us that when we had initially implemented IntheFlow, one of the guidelines was that we needed to send our responses to the administrator by 9.00 am every day. And so if this was the 'rule', why was it necessary to send the reminder in the first place?

Well, in theory she was absolutely correct. However, in practice, having the email reminder hanging in my inbox ensures that I do not get too distracted for too long without responding to the email, and it also allows me just to hit 'reply'!

It also means that when I or any of the team are on the road or not yet in the office, sending the email is as easy as can be.

And if there's one thing I've learnt, to create and sustain any kind of new ritual or habit, it needs to be done regularly. And one way to support regularity is simplicity.

Step 2: IntheFlow practice – the six prompts

As you now know (but to repeat, just in case something was missed earlier), this is your own, personal practice, which entails stopping for a few minutes to bring awareness to what's going on in your life. Scanning for Yesterday's Best Thing, becoming aware of what you're feeling Grateful For, and thinking about something you're Looking Forward To. Then, recalling (or reminding yourself to do) an act of Conscious Kindness, to Compliment Sincerely and to Greet Warmly.

And all of these thoughts and actions are then written down, and placed somewhere visible.

Step 3: The response

Now, what I'm going to present below is the way in which we do it at Jack Hammer. It works for us, but in other teams, with other contexts, you could (and should) adapt this to your own work environment.

In our team, 'the response' takes the form of a reply to the email reminder received from our office administrator.

And the reply includes only 'Yesterday's Best Thing' (which is our core, constant, every-day-without-fail element), and one additional element of IntheFlow.

So each day, after doing my personal IntheFlow practice (Step 2), I respond to the email reminder by typing my 'YBT', plus one other prompt. Which might be one of the remaining five elements (GF, LFT, CK, CS, GW), or something new that we add to make the whole process interesting and fun (read more about this later, in 'Keeping it Fresh').

Sometimes, my email is quite brief – one or two lines in bullet point. On other days, I have a slightly longer story to tell. The same goes for my team – it's typically one-liners from everyone, and then a couple of the good 'story-tellers' will go into a little more detail.

And then hit 'reply'.

NOT 'reply to all'. 'Reply-to-all's are mostly banned in my office, as they are terrible inbox cloggers!

Step 4: Collation and distribution of 'IntheFlow Report'

Our administrator collates the team's emails into one, and sends one 'IntheFlow Report' to the entire team, which arrives usually no later than 11.00 am.

One of the greatest pleasures of my day is reading this email. Here's an example:

Sarah	
YBT:	A really great coaching session with one of my coachees – realising that we're almost at the end of the process, and some real shifts have taken place. That's quite a wow for me, to see that the process really can make an impact in people's lives!
CK:	This was to myself – I have an incredibly busy schedule this week, and realised that in order to fit everything in, I need to re-prioritise and cancel a couple of things that I would LIKE to do, but are not essential – and by cancelling, I then make time for the important and urgent things that really need attention. This has eased my anxiety significantly around where to fit everything in!
Nikki	
YBT:	Getting home safely in the insane traffic and then getting to do homework with Sean. My youngest is now reading Sean's grade 2 books and loving it!
CK:	So many things can be said without saying a word and just by being attentive. I realised that a friend of mine was going through financial hardship – I immediately went to my grocery cupboards and started packing out groceries (porridge for her kids, milk, tinned goodies, rice and just everything). I am forever grateful for the fortunate situation I find myself in and know what it is like to be where my friend is right now. It wasn't too long ago – in gratitude always.

Anna

YBT: A short but refreshing post-work swim, followed by air-fried, SUPER spicy chicken wings.

CK: Well, it WAS going to be to bring some spicy wings in for Nikki but they were so good ... will have to think of something else today.

Gail

YBT: That moment when you realised that a shortlist is coming together ...

CK: Although a day late, I deposited a multiple of R67 in the bank account of Sedgefield's new animal rescue organisation.

Jillian

TBT: Reading our client's comments on our progress report. He actually read through every profile on the progress report and commented on the doc! What a super star.

CK: Leon is under a lot of pressure in his final year of school, and acting like a bit of a child, instead of being (rightfully) harsh with him I opted for kindness. The poor kid knows what needs to be done – no need for me to add to the pressure. He needs support not lectures.

Karen

YBT: As you can imagine while I'm staying at my mom's place, I'm being spoilt – got a warm cooked meal last night, (no cleaning the kitchen) and I had my dad entertaining the little one while I went to take a shower!

CK: My sister called for a chat about how crazy her upcoming weekend will be – with guests, work functions, events etc. I got the hint! Offered to take her kids for Saturday afternoon – sleepover Saturday night. Mine will be delighted. The kind part is that I offered without a 'then you take mine on ...'! Haha, I'm sure it'll come around!

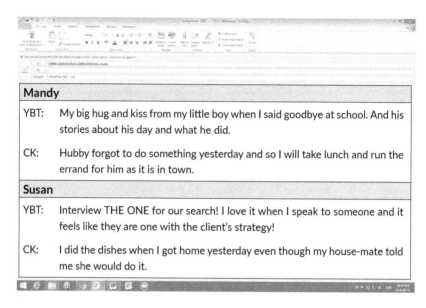

Mandy	
YBT:	My big hug and kiss from my little boy when I said goodbye at school. And his stories about his day and what he did.
CK:	Hubby forgot to do something yesterday and so I will take lunch and run the errand for him as it is in town.
Susan	
YBT:	Interview THE ONE for our search! I love it when I speak to someone and it feels like they are one with the client's strategy!
CK:	I did the dishes when I got home yesterday even though my house-mate told me she would do it.

I get to see what's been going on with my colleagues in their work and personal lives, and I have an opportunity to hear about stuff that would almost certainly have been missed had this forum not existed in this manner.

In particular, for those who work remotely (and these days, that's almost 40 – 50% of the team), the IntheFlow report is a vital link and connection to the pulse, energy, highlights (and lowlights) of what's going on with each team member.

But once the Report is sent – that's it. No email ping-ponging with responses and comments and quips ... even though it is very tempting to do so. Our IntheFlow Report guidelines are: no reply to all's, and no need to respond in any way to anyone's contribution (unless you really, really, really feel compelled to do so).

I will on occasion respond to something important or personal that has been shared by one of my colleagues, by calling or emailing ... but this is an exception. And it's quite liberating to share something, and then read everyone's contribution without feeling obliged to follow social niceties and respond in an 'appropriate' manner. No 'likes', no emoticons, nothing but taking in the words.

Which, in itself, is a great act of respect and appreciation.

25 Keeping it fresh

Interrelated with making IntheFlow work, is making sure that it doesn't become stale and boring. Which even this transformative, highly impactful programme will do if you don't keep it fresh and interesting.

I realised this after about a month of daily practice with my team.

We started off very excited at this new thing we were doing together, the energy was incredible, the daily IntheFlow Report was fabulous, and we were inspired and motivated.

For a while.

And then, as all new shiny things do, it lost its lustre a little and needed some polishing to keep the shine glowing.

So I decided to introduce something new each week, to shake things up a little, add some variety, try out some fun ideas and maintain the creative energy.

And I have to give my team credit for receiving some of my occasionally-odd or left-field ideas that I introduce each week at our company meeting (at Jack Hammer we only have one meeting a week – under an hour, 8.00 am sharp on a Monday), with good humour, open hearts and a willingness to give them a try.

The reason I mention the time of our weekly meeting is that it comes after I have completed my Monday morning 6.30 am workout, followed by my first flat white of the day (for those who don't know what this is ... it's a cappuccino in Cape Town). Meaning that I usually arrive at the meeting high on endorphins and caffeine.

So now I'm showing off a bit! I know it's not the handstand Olympics, but I was SO proud to be able to do a handstand – even one balancing on a wall – that I kept showing everyone in my office. This is what inspired the 'New Thing' exercise.
(Photo by Hetty Zantman)

IntheFlow is always at the end of the agenda, to close the meeting. We discuss which of the six prompts we'd like to focus on, or sometimes introduce a completely fresh idea that we'd like to bring awareness to during the week.

One Monday, I arrived at the meeting particularly juiced because I had for the first time ever in my life done a handstand during my morning workout. It may sound a little feeble, but for me this was incredible (yes, the handstand was assisted, and I did balance against a wall ... but I did it!). Something new that I had never done before, had never really contemplated doing and was actually a bit nervous about trying.

And then, once I had done it, I felt amazing … and rushed to my meeting higher than ever! I was inspired. If I had gained such a buzz out of doing something new, surely everyone in my team would love this too?

Well, I'm not sure whether they were all as entirely in love with the idea as I was, but that week, the task for each member of the team was to try something completely new that they had never ever ever done before. It could be anything. Play something, cook something, walk somewhere … anything new.

'The New Thing' was the first of our 'keeping it fresh' ideas, and it was a hit. At the end of the week, by 12 noon on Friday, each of us emailed a note on our 'New Thing' to our administrator who then collated it all and sent us all the consolidated 'New Thing' email.

I recall laughing, crying and being absolutely amazed and incredibly proud at what my team had achieved that week. They had embraced the 'New Thing' idea and had just gone for it! Not only are they great at putting heart and soul into everything they do … we also have some great story-tellers on board at Jack Hammer.

So the recollection of each one's 'New Thing' was truly something special … and very funny too. One of the team had gone on a blind date; another had baked a chocolate cake (she had never previously baked ANYTHING at all … she even had to go out to buy the pans, never mind the ingredients); another had taken a jog through the city centre at lunch time and landed up in a new 'nightclub' – in the middle of the day!

The 'New Thing' was just what we needed to invigorate IntheFlow, and from then onwards, we have become quite flexible and open to trying out some fun concepts, which any member of the team is free to introduce.

26 Nurturing Mindfulness –even in airports

The objective of the 'fresh' element we select for the week is to cultivate and nurture awareness – in one way or another. Ideally, it's something that can be undertaken daily, without any extra effort – other than turning on the awareness muscle.

Here are some examples of a few of our favourite ones:

Mindful Minute: The instruction for this exercise is to choose a minute – any minute – to 'switch on' awareness and attention, to experience things in a different way. This is a very directed Mindfulness-based exercise, which requires one to pay attention to our environment and the activity that we are busy with at the time – with specific cultivation of sensory awareness. The sounds, the sights, the smells, the way things feel as we go about our day. The feedback from the team on this one when we tried it out for the first time was 'totally awesome'!

Ordinary Little Thing:	A conscious awareness of the ordinary, routine moments of the day. By paying attention, we give these ordinary moments a figurative spotlight, bringing them into focus and thereby making them special. My 'Ordinary Little Thing' is usually something around my children; sometimes the lights of the city as I drive to work; or something that I notice in my garden. It could really be anything at all. The point of this exercise is to become conscious and present to all the beauty that surrounds us ... which we are not usually paying too much attention to, or which would otherwise go completely unnoticed and certainly unmentioned.
Breathing Break:	Although I am not overly evangelical about meditation (despite my own personal daily practice and belief in the extraordinary benefits of this ritual), the introduction of Breathing Break was an opportunity to try out a minute or two of focusing on the breath – during the middle of the work day – and observing ones physical, emotional or mental response.
My Mood:	This is a daily word or phrase describing your state of mind or how you feel – almost like an internal weather report. To do that, one obviously needs to become aware of how you're feeling. So not only is it an opportunity for a personal 'temperature check', it's also an excellent way to gauge the general energy levels and mood of the team.
I Learned:	Each day, we're learning new things. We're just not always conscious of these. So by focusing daily on something new (or old) that we learned, each one of us became very aware of the daily exposure and internalisation of information and learning.

Before Work I	We typically find ourselves on autopilot as we race to
Noticed:	the office or to our desks in our 'home-offices'. This
	exercise compels me to wake up from my mindless state
	and to become present to my surroundings. I find it really
	interesting to apply a different, more mindful awareness
	to the typical, regular events of the morning – what's
	happening in the traffic, what's new or different on
	my route to work, or what's going on with my morning
	routine at home as I hustle my kids to school.

During our first year of implementing IntheFlow, we probably introduced about twenty-five new ideas that we would try out on a weekly basis, to accompany 'Yesterday's Best Thing' in our daily IntheFlow report. Some worked better than others, but it is important to keep IntheFlow fresh, so it's totally ok if sometimes you try things that are a bit of a flop.

Frankly, I'm never quite sure about whether one of my 'inspirations' will work – but I'm always willing to give new ideas a try.

Like one Friday afternoon – I was at the airport returning from a meeting in Johannesburg, feeling great about something or another (maybe just life in general … the meeting must have gone well!), and while I was waiting to board I sent the team an email sharing my great energy and gratitude for how good life felt at that moment.

I then requested each one to take a few minutes to become aware of the joyful, positive, privileged aspects of their lives. Because even though it was Friday afternoon and it had been a tough and exhausting week for everyone, with some mini-dramas occurring with clients and candidates, causing anxiety all round (in other words, business as usual) – with some perspective, the work stress was actually quite small.

My second request was that, with that awareness in mind, each one in the team conduct either an act of Conscious Kindness or Compliment (someone) Sincerely, in order to 'pay it forward', so to speak, by the end of the day.

Now this may all sound a bit mushy and cushy. And perhaps it is. But I didn't really worry too much about whether anyone would roll their eyes at the 'suggestion'.

I sent the mushy-cushy email anyway, boarded my flight, and when I landed two hours later, turned on my phone which started beeping madly as emails downloaded. Including an email from each and every one of my team who, in the two hours while I'd been in the air, had completed the task!

What was so incredible about this was not just that they had grabbed the baton that I had handed over and run with it, but that they had actually made an impact on a whole lot of other people's lives. They had taken an idea, put it into action, carried the positive energy forward, and were rewarded in return because each one felt really fantastic for having done it.

I of course was in tears! (I cry a lot when I'm happy, as I think you know by now.)

All of this – the new weekly ideas, or the focus on one of the daily six, and even the random 'once-offs' (like 'New Thing'), are really important to keep IntheFlow alive, evolving and fresh.

Otherwise, like many other great concepts, it will lose momentum and energy, and ultimately wither into nothingness.

Don't let this happen!

And if it does, you'll eventually become aware of this – and then just begin again.

27 Taking IntheFlow back home

IntheFlow started as a big experiment. Collectively, with my 'work friends' as guinea pigs and lab rats.

Initially, it was mostly just a fun exercise (with the hope of positive outcomes). With time, it was clear that IntheFlow was having a much greater impact on all of our lives.

And the interesting thing about 'lives' is that it's pretty difficult to compartmentalise them. Yes, there's lots of theory on the separation of work and personal life (just think about the most prolific phrase on the topic: 'work-life balance'), and agreed, it is certainly possible to forget about stuff going on at home when work is particularly demanding or engrossing.

But we are all 'whole' people, and almost always, our stresses and anxieties spill over from the personal domain into the work one, and vice versa. And when things are going great in our personal or work lives, they tend to influence positively all round.

In the early days of practising IntheFlow, we started to see that the daily prompts were clearly impacting personal awareness – and once the awareness button was switched on, it stayed on (even temporarily) both in the office and at home.

The feedback from several staff members shows this in action.

One of the Jack Hammer senior consultants had this to say:

> 'The most beneficial aspect of IntheFlow has been in terms of my personal consciousness. I'm so much more aware of my mood, and of the things that give me pleasure. Anxiety is definitely lessened, and I've taken IntheFlow home, with very good effect. I'm more often seeking out the things that make me happy, letting fewer opportunities pass me by. Most importantly, I think IntheFlow has helped me to express my gratitude, appreciation, enjoyment, hopes and aspirations more clearly and with sincerity.'

And then this comment from a researcher:

> 'For me, I tend to take people for granted, and IntheFlow has certainly given me a lot of perspective in that regard. I have noticed a difference in the way I treat people, particularly my loved ones, and have become much more aware of the way that I interact with and treat them.'

Followed by this from one of our 'remoters' who lives on a farm on the Garden Route:

> 'Living in a rather remote area could breed loneliness and a tendency to be a hermit! Going through the IntheFlow prompts daily has not only made me keenly aware of the enormous positives of where and how I live, but also forced me (as an off-the-scale introvert) to integrate into my rural community and gain fulfilment in being able to make a difference in the lives of those who live around me.

'As a positive, upbeat personality by nature, this exercise has made me more aware of how fortunate I am, despite the bumps in the road. My life, or rather my perception of my life, and my experience of life, has become much lighter.'

Pretty great feedback and insight!

Yet despite this ongoing positive feedback from people who were practising IntheFlow daily, from time to time my sceptic's hat would plonk itself on my head, and I would question the validity of the team's responses. Was this in fact just a gimmicky idea, a quirky concept that was fun but possibly lacking in substance? Or was there actually something to it?

I finally chucked that hat in the trash for good after receiving an incredibly poignant note from one of my colleagues. This individual had endured an immensely challenging personal relationship over several years, which from time to time would feel quite overwhelming, despite being someone with an incredibly bright and cheery outlook on life.

This is what she said in the note:

> 'Some of the trials and tribulations that I have had to endure could weaken even the hardiest die-hard optimist! So the introduction of the IntheFlow exercise became a very real tool that I could use to cope on a day-to-day basis. In fact, it has become so ingrained as part of my daily life that I dream about what I'm looking forward to, wake up thinking about yesterday's best thing, and am constantly aware of opportunities throughout the day of being kind and nice and grateful.
>
> 'By becoming more aware of self, myself in my surroundings and how I can impact my surroundings (and the people who occupy that space), I've become independent of "what is", in other words largely unattached … and I don't have to be a victim of the choices I've made in my life.'

Finally, my sceptic's hat has been tossed!

28 The ripple effect – making the circle bigger

Now, it's one thing to gain real confidence in the substance and impact of IntheFlow. It's another to assess whether IntheFlow could exist beyond my company, without my personal input, leadership and motivation. Could it pass the test of sustainability, ease and simplicity with other groups of people?

This was still a question that needed some answers because if IntheFlow is an exercise that is so reliant on the unique features of Jack Hammer, then promoting it as a programme that can be used by others (that is, you) would just be false advertising!

Happily, the sustainability test has been passed, with other groups using (and adapting) IntheFlow with ease.

A member of the Jack Hammer team decided to start an IntheFlow group with her closest friends – who despite their friendship were not finding time to connect with one another as frequently as they would have liked, due to busy lives and not all living in the same city. And Facebook wasn't cutting it when it came to having a meaningful connection.

They call their group 'The Breakfast Club' and they have adapted IntheFlow to suit the needs of their friendship group:

> 'Based on the sense of togetherness that I've experienced with the daily practice of IntheFlow at work, my friends and I started practising ITF to ensure that we stay connected and know what's happening in each other's day-to-day lives. I was a bit worried that we wouldn't keep it up but it's become a highlight of our day.'

After a period, I received this note from my colleague, who had received some feedback from a 'Breakfast Club' member:

> 'I really love this daily touching base. It's really lovely knowing what is happening in your lives, sharing in your joys and excitement, as well as your worries or disappointments. Sharing things about myself also makes me take a few minutes to think about all my blessings and really be present. So, thank you.'

Now, I've never met this person. I do not know her, she doesn't know me, and she most certainly does not need to contribute this feedback to her friends for any reason other than genuine appreciation of the experience.

This was my first glimpse of seeing IntheFlow operate outside of Jack Hammer, and it encouraged me to start sharing the programme more proactively with other companies who had expressed a desire to enrich their team connection, or an interest in incorporating Mindfulness in their work environments.

One of the first companies I shared IntheFlow with, was a global consulting firm with offices in London, Cape Town and San Francisco. They decided to try an adapted version of IntheFlow, focusing on 'Yesterday's Best Thing' and 'Grateful For'.

As a company of people working remotely, they were keen to see if IntheFlow could benefit their team connection and influence their relationships positively – as well as whether the Mindfulness-based orientation would have some personal impact.

After a couple of months, they sent me some feedback on their experience with IntheFlow.

On the 'connection' aspect, they had this to say:

> 'IntheFlow helps us feel more connected as a team, and is especially useful since we are rarely in the same place at the same time. It also provides an opportunity to keep in touch with what is working and where our energy is.'

There was also commentary on the relational impact:

> 'It involves personal connection and integrates personal with work, which brings warmth to our interactions. It provides an opportunity to affirm one another, and also creates an equal playing ground for everyone, which is a good leveller in the team – it reduces hierarchy.'

Another contribution focusing on the 'sharing' element of IntheFlow noted this:

> 'It feels safe to share, because everyone is. It's either entertaining, heart-warming, reassuring or insightful reading what others have written, whether a personal or work sharing. And we get to know and understand each other better because of it.'

The group also noted the structured 'rules' of the exercise:

> 'Because no response, feedback or unsolicited advice is needed, it encourages honesty. You don't have to "like" someone's contribution to value it – it can just be. And because it's short and easy to read, it's not distracting or time-consuming. We want to read it.'

And a comment on how IntheFlow incorporates elements of Mindfulness captured it in a nutshell:

> 'It's a reminder of the value of being present. It feels good to reflect on what is important right now, and cuts to the heart of that.'

Air punch! Or to quote Higgins in *My Fair Lady*: 'By George, (they) got it!'

29 The unanticipated extra benefits

When I started practising IntheFlow on my own, the primary intention was to create a ritual that would help me to be more present, to become more aware of the 'here and now', and to cultivate an appreciation of all the small, ordinary moments that were happening in my day, but were not receiving much air time amongst the whining and moaning about how 'totally exhausted' I was.

As a very driven, output- and achievement-oriented person, I needed a strategy for stopping to smell the roses on the journey instead of being purely focused on getting to the end destination as swiftly as possible.

And I needed to wake up from the constant, unrelenting grind (mostly self-inflicted) of chasing one goal after the next, without pausing long enough to celebrate the achievements – or even the small moments along the way.

Now, I cannot tell you that all of a sudden I became a carefree, unstressed, totally joyful human being! Frankly, I'm still not that! However, without a doubt (even within the first month of practising IntheFlow) I felt a real shift in my attitude, approach and experience of not just work, but of my entire LIFE.

At work, we were having an incredible year: Jack Hammer experienced close to a 20% increase in turnover in the first year of practising IntheFlow – without any major additional infrastructure or resource costs. In fact, the payroll (and team size) stayed the same, my capital and infrastructure costs of the business were at similar levels to the previous year, and despite GDP growth declining nationally, revenue was way up!

But instead of feeling overwhelmed, overworked and exhausted (as I might have previously assumed would be the obvious outcome of business growth), I experienced the opposite. Counter-intuitively, my work hours and stress levels reduced by A LOT (granted, this is not a particularly quantitative assessment, but the sentiment and perception are actually what matters).

And so, because I had a bit (actually a lot) more time and energy, in the first year of IntheFlow I was able to take on some wonderfully exciting new projects outside of Jack Hammer. Notably, these included a facilitation training programme for a global entrepreneurship organisation (EO),[3] a dance project (which included my first professional stage performance in 15 years), several extraordinary travel adventures – including a momentous one to Nepal and a viewing (via helicopter) of Mount Everest together with Matthieu Ricard, and a surf trip to Maldives where I surfed the biggest wave of my life (so far).

---

3   EO is a global business network of 12 000+ entrepreneurs in 50 countries worldwide. I am a founding member of the Cape Town chapter, and a member of the Regional Council for the MEPA region (Middle East, Pakistan and Africa)

To some, this is a tiny wave. To me, this is a colossal monster. I was actually quite terrified to surf in the Maldives, but finally got the courage to get out there. Lots of air-punching afterwards.

My husband Zaheer and I on our trip to Nepal in March 2013. In the background is the peak of Everest. Extraordinary, awe-inspiring, and breath-taking.

2013 was the year I decided it was time to dance again. This piece, 'Rust Coloured Skirt', was performed at the main festival of the National Festival of the Arts in Grahamstown, and again at Artscape in Cape Town. (Photo by Mark Wessels)

So the fact that IntheFlow had an immediate impact on my entire life, by releasing TIME and ENERGY to take on some absolutely wonderful initiatives outside of day-to-day work was the first of the unanticipated benefits.

And this is a really fascinating point. If you had spoken to me a year earlier in my haggard state, I would have told you without any hesitation whatsoever that there was not one second more to do anything else AT ALL! The things going on in my life at the time were so all-consuming, that I could not possibly have believed that there would be room for anything else. And if I had tried to squeeze in something, it would no doubt have been met with resentment and irritation. With an attitude of having something else add to my 'load'.

How wonderfully refreshing to find that with a less burdened and stressed-out mind, with a lighter, easier approach, with tools to help me stop and 'smell the flowers' and appreciate bits of even the most challenging days – I was all of a sudden finding the space and time to take on more!

And whereas 'more' would have felt absolutely awful in the past, 'more' was now met with excitement and anticipation.

I can explain this only by taking a look at the one big change that had taken place during this period:

Mindfulness practice – through meditation and IntheFlow.

The second, quite extraordinary, already-mentioned upside, was that our daily IntheFlow Report proved to be an outstanding tool for connecting the team. No need for 'team-building events', and no need for 'team talks'. What the IntheFlow Report did for our team was quite extraordinary.

Without fail, when asked about what they love most about IntheFlow, each and every member of the Jack Hammer team commented (and you've read the feedback already) that it provides a great way to feel connected with one another. In particular with all of the 'remoters' who are deprived of the tangible energy that one encounters when you're physically in the Jack Hammer office.

The connection, the culture of 'love and loyalty', empathy and compassion that has arisen amongst my group of 'work friends' was not anticipated at all – but is undoubtedly one of the best outcomes of IntheFlow. A great gift that none of us were expecting, and which we have received with gratitude.

30 Off you go!

OK, it's the last chapter – you made it! Pat on the back to you ... and to me (I've managed to keep your attention for this long!).

Now, just because you've read the book all the way to the end, and have some very practical tools to start your daily IntheFlow practice, does not mean that all of a sudden everything is going to change.

Firstly, it apparently takes 90 days of consecutive practice to create or change a habit. I don't recall where I picked up this piece of behavioural psychology trivia, but in my experience, it's about right.

And, despite your exceptional display of tenacity in the reading department, I understand and empathise if you're now wondering how on earth you're going to get out of the starting blocks and actually do this thing. It may feel a bit like reading about how to swim, and now standing at the edge of the pool, right?

So, let's go slow and easy.

Start with writing down the list:

YBT:	Yesterday's Best Thing
GF:	Grateful For
LFT:	Looking Forward To
CK:	Conscious Kindness
GW:	Compliment Sincerely
CS:	Greet Warmly

Then, imagine how you might feel if you were able to stop, and bring awareness to each one of these prompts every single day.

How would things be if you started your day noticing yesterday's best moments; becoming aware of feelings of gratitude (and then making contact with someone to acknowledge your appreciation); stopping to think about something that you are looking forward to today; practising conscious kindness to others (or yourself); sincerely complimenting others; and greeting the people around you with warmth and attentiveness?

I'll speak for myself, and say without any shadow of a doubt, a day like this which includes moments of mindful awareness feels pretty remarkable. A day when I am present and 'awake' and not operating on automatic makes me feel invigorated and energised.

A day like this is really how I want to continue to live my life.

And now it's over to YOU.

I hope you're ready to give it a go. I mean, now that you've read this far, surely there's no turning back? Think about the effort you've just put into reading all these sentences to get to this point.

You can do it.

One step at a time (well, actually six).

Just think ... what was Yesterday's Best Thing? ...

ENDNOTES

1   Rilke, 1929.
2   Penman & Williams, 2011.
3   Kabat-Zinn, 2013.
4   Kabat-Zinn, 2006.
5   Kabat-Zinn, 1994.
6   Tang, 2007.
7   Tang, 2009.
8   Davidson, Kabat-Zinn, Schumacher, Rosenkranz, Muller, Santorelli, Urbanowski, Harrington, Bonus, & Sheridan, 2003.
9   Robbins.
10 Tracy, 2004.
11 Canfield, & Hansen, 2008.
12 Lutz, Greischar, Rawlings, Ricard, & Davidson, 2004.
13 Bates, 2012.
14 Hanh, 2008.
15 Tan, 2014.
16 Wikimedia, 2016.
17 Kabat-Zinn, 2013.
18 Emmons, 2007.
19 Emmons, 2013.
20 Achor, May 2011.
21 Gutman, March 2011.

BIBLIOGRAPHY

Achor, S. May 2011. 'The happy secret to better work'. *TED.* [Online] Available: https://www.ted.com/talks/shawn_achor_the_happy_secret_to_better_work?language=en [Accessed 19 September 2016].

Bates, C. 2012. 'What is Your Weakest Chakra? Is this the world's happiest man? Brain scans reveal French monk has "abnormally large capacity" for joy – thanks to meditation'. *DailyMail.* 31 October 2012. [Online] Available. http://www.dailymail.co.uk/health/article-2225634/Is-worlds-happiest-man-Brain-scans-reveal-French-monk-abnormally-large-capacity-joy-meditation.html [Accessed 19 September 2016].

Canfield, J. & Hansen M. V. 2008. *Chicken Soup for the Soul: Living Catholic Faith.* New York: Simon & Schuster.

Davidson, R. J., Kabat-Zinn, J., Schumacher, J., Rosenkranz, M. A., Muller, D., Santorelli, S. F., Urbanowski, F., Harrington, A., Bonus, K., & Sheridan, J. F. 2003. Alterations in brain and immune function produced by mindfulness meditation. *Psychosomatic Medicine,* 65, 564-570.

Emmons, R. 2007. *Thanks!: How the New Science of Gratitude Can Make You Happier.* New York: Houghton Mifflin Harcourt.

Emmons, R. 2013. *Gratitude Works!: A 21-Day Program for Creating Emotional Prosperity.* San Francisco, CA: Jossey-Bass.

Gutman, R. March 2011. 'The hidden power of smiling' *TED.* [Online] Available: https://www.ted.com/talks/ron_gutman_the_hidden_power_of_smiling?language=en [Accessed 19 September 2016].

Hanh, T. N. 2008. *Work: How to Find Joy and Meaning in Each Hour of the Day.* Berkeley, CA: Parallax Press.

Kabat-Zinn, J. 1994. *Wherever You Go, There You Are.* New York: Hyperion.

Kabat-Zinn, J. 2006. *Mindfulness for Beginners.* Audio CD – Audiobook, CD, Unabridged. Louisville : USA. Sounds True.

Kabat-Zinn, J. 2013. *Full Catastrophe Living: Using the Wisdom of Your Body and Mind to Face Stress, Pain, and Illness.* New York: USA. Bantam Dell Publishing Group, Div of Random House, Inc.

Lutz, A., Greischar, L. L., Rawlings, N. B., Ricard, M. & Davidson, R. J. August 26, 2004. 'Long-term meditators self-induce high-amplitude gamma synchrony during mental practice'. *PNAS (Proceedings of the National Academy of Sciences of the United States of America).* [Online] Available: http://www.pnas.org/content/101/46/16369.long [Accessed 19 September 2016].

Rilke M. R. to Franz Xaver Kappus (Paris, 17 February 1903), compiled as the first letter in Rilke, Rainer Maria. *Letters to a Young Poet* (1929).

Rilke, R. M. & Kappus, F. X. 1993. *Letters to a Young Poet* in an edition by M.D. Herter Norton (translator). New York: W. W. Norton & Co., 1993.

Robbins, T. 'RPM Life Management System: Rapid planning method, results focused life planner'. San Diego, CA. Robbins Research International, Inc. [Online] Available: https://www.tonyrobbins.com/products/productivity-performance/rpm-life-planner/ [Accessed 19 September 2016].

Tan C-M. 2014. *Search Inside Yourself: The Unexpected Path to Achieving Success, Happiness.* London: HarperOne.

Tang Y. Y., et al. 2007. Short-term meditation training improves attention and self-regulation. *Proceedings of the National Academy of Sciences of the United States of America,* 104, 17152–17156.

Tang Y. Y., et al. 2009. Central and autonomic nervous system interaction is altered by short-term meditation. *Proceedings of the National Academy of Sciences of the United States of America,* 106, 8865–8870.

Tracy, B. 2004. *Goals!: How to Get Everything You Want Faster Than You Ever Thought Possible.* San Francisco: Berrett-Koehler Publishers.

Wikimedia. 2016. 'Ronald David Laing'. [Online] Available: https://en.wikiquote.org/wiki/Ronald_David_Laing [Accessed 19 September 2016].

Williams, M. & Penman, D. 2011. *Mindfulness: A practical guide to finding peace in a frantic world.* London: Piatkus.

CPSIA information can be obtained
at www.ICGtesting.com
Printed in the USA
BVHW04s0246151018
529909BV00009B/750/P